# The
# Successful
# Paraprofessional

How to Make a

Difference Supporting

Students and Teachers

KRISTEN NELSON

Solution Tree | Press

*a division of*
Solution Tree

555 North Morton Street
Bloomington, IN 47404
800.733.6786 (toll free) / 812.336.7700
FAX: 812.336.7790

email: info@SolutionTree.com
SolutionTree.com

Visit **go.SolutionTree.com/instruction** to download the free reproducibles in this book.

Printed in the United States of America

FSC
www.fsc.org
MIX
Paper | Supporting
responsible forestry
FSC® C008955

Library of Congress Cataloging-in-Publication Data

Names: Nelson, Kristen author
Title: The successful paraprofessional : how to make a difference
    supporting students and teachers / Kristen Nelson.
Description: Bloomington, IN : Solution Tree Press, [2026] | Includes
    bibliographical references and index.
Identifiers: LCCN 2025029505 (print) | LCCN 2025029506 (ebook) | ISBN
    9781962188876 paperback | ISBN 9781962188883 ebook
Subjects: LCSH: Teachers' assistants
Classification: LCC LB2844.1.A8 N39 2026  (print) | LCC LB2844.1.A8
    (ebook) | DDC 371.1--dc23/eng/20251215
LC record available at https://lccn.loc.gov/2025029505
LC ebook record available at https://lccn.loc.gov/2025029506

**Solution Tree**
Cameron L. Rains, CEO
Edmund M. Ackerman, President

**Solution Tree Press**
*Publisher:* Kendra Slayton
*Associate Publisher:* Todd Brakke
*Acquisitions Director:* Hilary Goff
*Editorial Director:* Laurel Hecker
*Art Director:* Rian Anderson
*Managing Editor:* Sarah Ludwig
*Copy Chief:* Jessi Finn
*Senior Production Editor:* Suzanne Kraszewski
*Proofreader:* Charlotte Jones
*Text and Cover Designer:* Laura Cox
*Content Development Specialist:* Amy Rubenstein
*Associate Editor:* Elijah Oates
*Editorial Assistant:* Madison Chartier

*To all the superhero paraprofessionals who make an incredible difference in the lives of children every day—your unwavering dedication and compassion are truly heroic.*

*To my superhero parents, daughters, and friends, who are always there to support me—your love and encouragement make everything possible.*

# Acknowledgments

I want to acknowledge the incredible team at Solution Tree who made this book possible. Thank you to Claudia Wheatley for believing in the book and believing it needed to be written. Thank you to Laurel Hecker and Suzanne Kraszewski for being excellent editors and encouragers. I also greatly appreciate the paraprofessionals I asked for advice and wisdom, especially those in Plymouth, Indiana. Working with superheroes is humbling and exciting, and I will be forever grateful to contribute a book to these incredible educators.

Solution Tree Press would like to thank the following reviewers:

Lorraine Atwater
   Paraeducator
   Hastings Middle School
   Hastings, Nebraska

John D. Ewald
   Associate
   Solution Tree
   Frederick, Maryland

Kimberly Mellon
   Special Education Paraprofessional
   Onalaska Middle School
   Onalaska, Wisconsin

Visit **go.SolutionTree.com/instruction** to download the free reproducibles in this book.

# Table of Contents

*Reproducibles are in italics.*

# About the Author

**Kristen Nelson** is an elementary school principal for the Capistrano Unified School District in California. She has been the principal of several elementary schools, as well as the district's executive director of state and federal programs. Kristen is also a professor at Concordia University Irvine and teaches leadership courses for the Contra Costa County and Orange County departments of education. In 2025, she was named Elementary Principal of the Year in the Capistrano Unified School District.

Kristen began her career as a paraprofessional. She fell in love with the job, working daily with students in a special needs classroom and being in the education arena. That love has never ceased, and she now contributes to the field of education that has given her so much as an educational consultant. She provides support and assistance to education administration programs throughout the state of California. She is a frequent guest lecturer and assists with overall program design.

Kristen is the author of several books, including *Starting Strong: Surviving and Thriving as a New Teacher*; *Teaching in the Cyberage: Linking the Internet and Brain Theory*; and *Developing Students' Multiple Intelligences, Grades K–8*. She is coauthor with Kim Bailey of *The Successful Substitute: How to Prepare, Grow, and Flourish as a Guest Teacher*.

Kristen earned a bachelor of science in child psychology from the University of California, Santa Barbara, where she was also an NCAA Division I basketball player. She also earned a master's degree in education from California State University, Fullerton.

To learn more about Kristen's work, visit her LinkedIn page (www.linkedin.com /in/kristenjnelson88).

To book Kristen Nelson for professional development, contact pd@ SolutionTree.com.

# Preface

I was three months out of college and living in Santa Barbara, California, unsure of what I was going to do with my life or career. I had odd jobs to pay the rent but didn't have a plan for my life. I knew one thing for sure, though: I was not going to go into education. Nope! My mom and dad were both teachers at the high school I attended, and that was enough to convince me; even though they greatly enjoyed their jobs, I just felt like I should do something different.

So, I went on a career search, and I found some interesting prospects. Maybe I would become a psychologist or a physical therapist. Meanwhile, rent was not getting cheaper, and I needed to find a higher-paying job. A friend's dad suggested I apply as a paraprofessional to the local school district. I almost laughed out loud at that suggestion, but out of respect, I held it together and promised him I would look into it. He was a principal in the district, and he left me with these words: "It is meaningful work, Kristen. You never know; you may just like it."

Five weeks later, I walked into an elementary special needs classroom as a paraprofessional. I had no clue what I was doing. I could not believe the school trusted me around people's children! As the weeks turned into months, I began figuring out the job with the help of the classroom teacher and students. I was a one-on-one paraprofessional with a student with Tourette's syndrome. My main responsibility, as it was explained to me, was to always be close to my student and make sure she did not swear at younger students or hurt anyone when she became upset. As time went on, I acquired other responsibilities in the classroom and with my student. No two days were the same; as soon as I thought I understood my student, she would surprise me. Luckily, as a former Division I basketball player who had to be an adaptable and flexible team player with a positive mindset, I was up to the task.

I found the rhythm, sights, and sounds of a busy school comforting and always interesting. Sometimes, I felt lost among the other staff members—like I didn't belong. However, the staff were kind to me, and I knew I belonged in my classroom. When the school year was coming to an end, I felt a sadness I did not expect. I was going to miss my student, the other students, and the classroom environment. My parents suggested I go back to school to get a teaching credential. In considering this suggestion, I realized that my reluctance to go into education had not just softened but disappeared. I entered an education program the following fall, and the rest is history. I absolutely loved teaching, and I also love being a principal. I am thankful my paraprofessional role opened the door to such a rewarding and fulfilling career.

From paraprofessional to principal—that is an interesting journey and one that has humbled me in many ways. When I encounter paraprofessionals within my school, I warmly greet them; I remember how challenging—and rewarding—their job is. I want them to know that they are appreciated, they are seen, and they belong. I have had the opportunity to know many amazing paraprofessionals (like my mom, who also started as a paraprofessional) throughout my career. As the years have gone by, I have found myself calling them my superheroes, and I mean it.

My journey from paraprofessional to principal inspired me to write this book. I wish there had been more support and training for paraprofessionals when I first began my career many years ago; I believe that this area of the education field can be improved. Paraprofessionals are a critical part of a successful school. This book is for the superheroes: the retired ones who led the way, the current ones who are doing amazing work, and the future ones who will carry our education system forward. We are lucky to have you!

# A Guide for Paraprofessionals

The classroom is a dynamic environment where teachers, armed with knowledge, strive to inspire a diverse group of learners. Amid the chaos and excitement, heroes emerge; one is the superhero paraprofessional, navigating the complexities of the classroom, supporting students with challenging needs, and contributing to an effective learning environment.

Paraprofessionals serve as one-on-one tutors and act as classroom managers. They collaborate with teachers to implement effective teaching strategies, celebrate student victories big and small, and provide individualized support to the students who need it most.

> Amid the chaos and excitement, heroes emerge; one is the superhero paraprofessional.

This book will guide you to discover your full potential as a paraprofessional and embrace your critical role in shaping young minds. It will explore the challenges, celebrate the triumphs, and equip you with the tools you need to begin or continue your superhero journey. In this introduction, you'll gain a preview of the topics and structure of the book, as well as the inspiration and practical insights that will ground your learning in the chapters ahead. Think of this book as your launchpad for the exciting, rewarding, and essential work of being a paraprofessional.

## Elevating the Role of the Superhero Paraprofessional

In detailing all the important aspects of the paraprofessional role, this book also celebrates the invaluable contributions of paraprofessionals: the essential skills they possess, the classroom management techniques they use, and their strategies for collaborating effectively with teachers. Understanding diverse learning needs and working with a wide range of students are second nature to the paraprofessional. Real-world examples, case studies, and practical tips from successful superhero paraprofessionals will bring these concepts to life. By the end of the journey of this book, you'll be armed with the knowledge and confidence to become a superhero paraprofessional.

This book demonstrates a mission to elevate the important role of the educational paraprofessional. As we work together throughout this book, we'll improve not just your experience but the academic journey of all your students. Being a paraprofessional means working with students who are struggling to get through their days. With your help and dedication, these students can experience more academic success and get a different view of their abilities and skills to successfully live and function in this world. That is one big mission!

## Making a Difference as Proven by Research

How can we compare paraprofessionals and superheroes? How can we not? Here are some reasons why this is a perfect comparison.

- **Both are quick to come to the rescue:** Paraprofessionals work alongside teachers, providing them with critical support and backup in the classroom. They anticipate needs, defuse situations, and empower teachers to deliver powerful lessons.

- **Both have the power of organization:** Paraprofessionals possess incredible skills. While superheroes utilize their utility belts, paraprofessionals keep track of materials, schedules, and student progress to ensure that resources are ready and available and everything runs smoothly.

- **Both are masters of adaptation:** Paraprofessionals can quickly adapt their strategies to the ever-changing and unpredictable classroom. They think on their feet, solve problems creatively, and handle unexpected situations with a smile.

- **Both put their shields up:** Paraprofessionals act as shields for students, protecting them from distractions that can affect learning. They provide individual support, manage behavior, and create a safe, welcoming space where every student can thrive.

- **Both are empathetic and understanding:** Paraprofessionals connect with students on an authentic level. They actively listen, celebrate achievements, and offer encouragement.

- **Both unlock others' potential:** Paraprofessionals see beyond challenges and can focus on hidden strengths in each student. By providing support and differentiated instruction, they help students reach their full potential academically, socially, and emotionally.

- **Both embrace teamwork:** Superheroes and paraprofessionals do not operate alone. Paraprofessionals collaborate with teachers, administrators, and other professionals to form a powerful team dedicated to student success.

Studies show that paraprofessionals are more than just helpers; they're catalysts for student success. A study by the Institute of Education Sciences (Garcia, 2021) shows the benefits of hiring more paraprofessionals. Paraprofessionals boost student achievement, particularly for students of color. Paraprofessionals' impact extends beyond academics as well. The study finds that trained paraprofessionals can significantly improve student outcomes, from reducing behavior problems to increasing independence for students with disabilities (Garcia, 2021).

This job is important, and you are important! Research shows that paraprofessionals make a huge difference in students' lives and that an investment in paraprofessionals is well worth it. Table I.1 shares research that backs up the importance of this superhero job.

**Table I.1: Research Studies on the Effectiveness of Paraprofessionals**

| Research Study | Study Findings |
| --- | --- |
| Garcia (2021) | Paraeducators positively impact students' reading and mathematics achievement scores on standardized tests, with powerful effects on students of color. The study suggests that hiring additional paraeducators could be a cost-effective strategy for improving student test scores. |
| Walker, Douglas, Douglas, and D'Agostino (2020) | When given training, paraprofessionals can effectively implement several educational practices that improve academic and social outcomes, reduce problem behaviors, and increase independence for students with disabilities. |
| Thompson and Kirkwood (2021) | Paraprofessionals are integral to the learning and growth of students with unique needs, but they need ongoing training. |
| Florio (2024) | Paraprofessionals play a crucial role in ensuring a thriving learning environment and helping students reach their full potential. |
| Education 360 Journal (2024) | Paraprofessional support is associated with positive outcomes for students with disabilities. Paraprofessionals' involvement can improve academic performance and social integration. |
| Jones, Erchul, and Geraghty (2021) | Paraprofessionals as reading interventionists are highly promising practitioners for increasing student achievement. |

These research studies illuminate how paraprofessionals get amazing results when working with a wide range of students. This is not surprising when you consider the many flexible superpowers a paraprofessional is equipped to use each day.

## Unlocking Your Full Potential

This book is your guide to overcoming challenges and unlocking your full potential as a paraprofessional. Get ready to embrace your strengths and step into your role with confidence. Inside these pages, you'll explore the key skills that set exceptional paraprofessionals apart—from fostering meaningful connections with students to mastering effective classroom strategies.

Together, we have the power to elevate the role of paraprofessionals and create lasting, positive change in education. This book isn't just a resource—it's a movement. Let's inspire young minds, strengthen our classrooms, and build more supportive learning communities. The journey starts now. Here's what you'll find in each chapter.

> This book isn't just a resource—it's a movement. Let's inspire young minds, strengthen our classrooms, and build more supportive learning communities.

### Being a Successful Paraprofessional

Chapter 1 presents the wide variety of paraprofessional opportunities, highlighting the many paths you can take to make a meaningful impact in education. You'll explore various roles, from one-on-one support superheroes to classroom management magicians, and discover options that align with your unique skills and interests. Beyond the job description, you'll uncover the hidden rewards of being a paraprofessional—like the joy of witnessing student growth and the deep fulfillment of playing a vital role in students' learning journeys. We'll also dive into the key traits that make paraprofessionals shine, from razor-sharp organizational skills to an unwavering can-do spirit. Finally, we'll walk through a paraprofessional's typical workday to prepare you for both the challenges and the rewarding moments—big and small—that come with working alongside students.

### Developing a Paraprofessional Mindset

Imagine having a secret weapon—a set of skills that make you an invaluable asset in the classroom. Chapter 2 equips you with just that. You will learn the ten essential characteristics of a superhero paraprofessional based on information from experienced educators and research. You will be reminded of the importance of having a growth mindset and continuing to grow and challenge yourself. This chapter will also provide ideas for how you can collaborate with other professionals and play an essential role in learning communities.

### *Supporting Diverse Learners*

Any classroom is a rich tapestry of students, each with unique needs and learning preferences. Chapters 3–6 equip you with the tools to become a champion for every student.

- **Being an ally for students with special needs:** In chapter 3, you will learn how to navigate Individualized Education Programs (IEPs), unlock effective strategies for working with students with special needs, and become a trusted partner in a student's educational journey. The chapter discusses different types of disabilities, as well as the continuum of services for working with special needs students.

- **Supporting students with behavioral and attention challenges:** Chapter 4 explores positive and proactive approaches to managing challenging behaviors, building student connections, and creating a calm and focused learning environment. Behavior is a way that students communicate, and once you learn to speak their language, their behavior may quickly improve.

- **Becoming a champion for social-emotional well-being:** Students face increasing social and emotional challenges. Chapter 5 equips you with the tools to support their social-emotional and mental health. Discover practical strategies and social-emotional learning activities to foster resilience and well-being in students. You will discern how to work with students who have experienced trauma and help them get back to learning through understanding and connection.

- **Supporting students with learning challenges:** Chapter 6 will help you master various instructional strategies to empower students with learning difficulties. Learn to reteach, recast lessons, and assess student progress to become a true advocate for academic success. Also included in this chapter are information and resources to help you work with students who are struggling to learn English as an additional language.

### *Serving as the Primary Educator*

Sometimes, the unexpected happens. Chapter 7 equips you with the knowledge and confidence to navigate situations where you might be leading the classroom. Learn how to ensure a smooth and consistent student learning experience even when the primary teacher is absent.

*Attending to Self-Care and Continuing to Grow*

Being a superhero requires self-care. Chapter 8 unveils practical tips for nourishing your physical, mental, emotional, and spiritual well-being. This chapter also explores the importance of lifelong learning and provides resources to help you grow as a paraprofessional.

Each chapter features a relevant case study to learn from, an Advice From Superhero Paraprofessionals section, and a reproducible "Notes and Reflections" tool designed to deepen your understanding and help you apply what you've learned. These features connect theory to practice, provide real-world perspectives, and give you space to reflect, plan, and grow with intention.

## Getting Started

Thank you for choosing this incredible journey of self-discovery and advocacy. Your impact on students' lives is immeasurable. Let's celebrate your dedication with support, growth opportunities, and the recognition you deserve. Together, we can make a world of difference in education.

This book is for aspiring paraprofessionals, paraprofessionals currently in training, and seasoned paraprofessionals looking to deepen their skills. It's also a valuable resource for college students in education programs, classroom teachers, and school leaders seeking to better understand and support the vital work of paraprofessionals. Are you ready to embark on this exciting journey? Let's get started!

# Being a Superhero Paraprofessional

**1**

Being a paraprofessional is a rewarding job. One of its most rewarding aspects is that you play a crucial role in supporting students' learning and overall well-being, which has a profound impact on their lives. The work is inherently meaningful; it provides a sense of purpose and fulfillment because it directly contributes to students' educational development and success. The role also offers a significant opportunity for growth, with many paraprofessionals using the job as a stepping stone for further education or training in the field.

This chapter explores the reasons for being a paraprofessional, the many roles of a paraprofessional, realistic expectations, and requirements, as well as the onboarding experience and etiquette.

## Reasons to Be a Paraprofessional

As a paraprofessional, making a difference in students' lives means you get to witness students blossom, celebrate their achievements, and feel

### KEY POINTS

- Understand that being a paraprofessional means making a difference in students' lives and being part of a school community.

- Realize that paraprofessionals have many roles within schools.

- Recognize the various requirements and expectations for being a paraprofessional.

a sense of purpose that comes with helping them learn and grow. Here are nine incredible rewards of being a paraprofessional.

1. **You make a lasting impact:** Your influence goes far beyond academics. You help shape students' self-confidence and emotional well-being. Whether you're supporting a struggling reader or offering calm in a moment of crisis, your presence truly changes lives.

2. **You grow professionally every day:** This hands-on role sharpens key skills like classroom management, behavioral support, communication, and organization. You constantly learn new instructional strategies, technology tools, and insights into how students learn—valuable information that translates to many future career paths.

3. **You're part of a powerful team:** Paraprofessionals are essential collaborators. You work alongside teachers, administrators, and specialists to create effective, supportive learning environments. Your voice matters, and your teamwork fuels student success.

4. **You build deep, meaningful relationships:** The bonds you form with students are often lifelong. Many look to you for encouragement, guidance, and trust, and they'll remember your impact for years to come.

5. **You bring joy and pride to your work:** Few jobs let people feel immediate joy and pride from the results of their efforts. Watching a student succeed because of your support is incredibly fulfilling, whether you see them mastering a skill, growing in confidence, or managing emotions more effectively.

6. **You have flexibility and stability:** Paraprofessional roles often offer flexible schedules and school-year calendars that align with family life. Meanwhile, rising student needs have created a demand for skilled paraprofessionals across districts and increased paraprofessionals' job security.

7. **You're part of a vibrant school community:** A school is a lively, energetic place where you can participate in events from spirit days to assemblies; celebrate milestones; and help shape a positive culture. This is a job full of heart, energy, and celebration.

8. **You champion inclusion and diversity:** You work with students who are neurodiverse and who come from diverse cultural and socioeconomic backgrounds. Your role in fostering a respectful, inclusive classroom helps every student feel seen, valued, and supported.

9. **You strengthen your community:** By working in local schools, you become a trusted presence in the lives of students and families. Your work builds community connections and leaves a legacy that stretches far beyond the classroom.

As you can see, this job is full of rewards and opportunities. Education is always evolving, and paraprofessionals grow alongside it. Every day is an opportunity to learn from the students you serve, the educators you collaborate with, and the new strategies you explore. If you're curious and committed to continuous improvement, this role will keep you inspired for years to come. Are you ready to make a difference and accept your mission? The next section explores the various roles of paraprofessionals.

> Your influence goes far beyond academics. You help shape students' self-confidence and emotional well-being. Your presence truly changes lives.

## The Many Roles of a Paraprofessional

There's no one-size-fits-all paraprofessional role. You might work one-on-one with students who need extra support, help teachers manage lively classrooms, or even assist with special projects. The variety keeps things interesting. You can often apply for a specific type of paraprofessional job, but sometimes, the school may ask you to be flexible and fill different paraprofessional roles. The types of jobs you may encounter include the following.

- **Instructional paraprofessional:** Instructional paraprofessionals are vital for ensuring all students receive the support they need to succeed academically. They assist teachers with classroom instruction by working with individual students or small groups of students who need extra reinforcement. In classrooms with a high student-to-teacher ratio, they help manage the workload to ensure all students receive attention. Additionally, they may support behavior management strategies, reinforce lesson objectives, and provide interventions as directed by the teacher. Since their daily schedule is flexible, they must be adaptable and ready to jump in where support is most needed.

- **Special education paraprofessional:** Special education paraprofessionals work closely with students with disabilities, help implement Individualized Education Programs, and provide necessary accommodations. They may work in a general education setting, where they assist with student inclusion, or in specialized classrooms designed for students with more significant support needs. Their role can involve assisting with academics, behavioral intervention plans, personal care, mobility support, and communication. A strong understanding of patience, empathy, and adaptive teaching strategies is crucial in this role. (See chapter 3 for more information on adaptive teaching strategies.)

- **Bilingual or multilingual paraprofessional:** Language barriers can be significant obstacles for English learners (ELs), and bilingual or multilingual paraprofessionals bridge those gaps. They work closely with students who are learning English, helping them understand lesson content, develop language skills, and build confidence in the classroom. They typically provide their support within the general education setting to ensure that EL students can access the curriculum while improving their English proficiency. (See chapter 6 for more information.)

- **Library paraprofessional:** For those who love books and literacy, being a library paraprofessional is a rewarding position. These individuals assist librarians with cataloging books, maintaining an organized library space, and guiding students to select reading materials. They often help foster a love of reading by organizing book fairs, literacy events, and read-aloud sessions. Though these positions are uncommon, they provide excellent opportunities to promote literacy and learning.

- **Classroom behavioral support paraprofessional:** Behavioral support paraprofessionals play a critical role in helping students with social-emotional and behavioral challenges succeed in school. They work closely with students who have behavioral intervention plans and help them regulate their emotions, develop coping strategies, and engage appropriately in classroom activities. While they primarily provide support in the general education setting, they may also assist in special education classrooms or pull-out programs designed to support behavior management. This role requires patience, consistency, and a strong understanding of positive behavior reinforcement strategies. (See chapter 4 and chapter 5.)

- **Technology or science, technology, engineering, and mathematics (STEM) paraprofessional:** Technology and STEM paraprofessionals support students and teachers in effectively using technology as an integral part of education. They assist with computer-based learning, troubleshoot technical issues, and help implement STEM-related projects in subjects like coding, robotics, and engineering. Their role is essential in ensuring students gain the technological literacy needed in today's digital world.

- **Physical education paraprofessional:** For those who enjoy an active role, physical education paraprofessionals assist with organizing and supervising physical education activities. They help set up equipment, ensure student safety during physical exercises, and support students who need accommodations to participate in activities. Since some physical education teachers travel between schools, physical education paraprofessionals are crucial in keeping lessons organized and ensuring smooth transitions between activities.

- **Speech or occupational therapy paraprofessional:** Paraprofessionals in this role work alongside speech-language pathologists or occupational therapists to support students with speech delays, communication disorders, or motor-skill challenges. They assist in therapy sessions, help implement individualized treatment plans, and provide extra practice on skills outside of direct therapy time. These positions require a strong understanding of therapeutic interventions and patience in working with students with specific needs.

- **Mathematics or reading specialist paraprofessional:** Students who struggle with foundational skills in mathematics or reading often need additional support, which is where these paraprofessionals come in. They work with students in small groups or one-on-one, reinforcing concepts taught in the classroom and providing targeted interventions. They may support students in special education settings or within general education classrooms to ensure struggling learners don't fall behind. Their role is crucial in helping students build confidence and competence in core academic areas. (See chapter 6 for more information.)

- **Art or music paraprofessional:** Art and music bring creativity and self-expression into education, and paraprofessionals in these areas help support engaging lessons. They assist teachers in organizing materials, setting up classrooms, and guiding students through creative projects. Since many art and music teachers travel between schools, these paraprofessionals help ensure lessons run smoothly by keeping supplies organized and providing hands-on support during activities.

- **Early childhood education paraprofessional:** Supporting young learners in preschool or early childhood programs requires patience, energy, and an understanding of child development. Early childhood paraprofessionals assist teachers with hands-on learning activities, social-emotional development, and foundational academic skills. They help children navigate routines, engage in structured play, and build early literacy and mathematics skills. This role is essential as early childhood education expands, providing crucial support in preparing young learners for future academic success.

These roles can vary based on the school's specific needs and the paraprofessional's qualifications and skills. The job of a paraprofessional can mean juggling a lot of different roles. Let's consider a paraprofessional in an elementary school who is supporting a classroom of students with varied abilities and needs.

The paraprofessional may start the day by assisting a student with special needs, providing one-on-one support to help them navigate morning routines and settle into the classroom environment. This involves academic support and emotional reassurance to ensure a smooth transition. As the day progresses, the paraprofessional might shift roles to assist the teacher with classroom management during a group activity. This could involve helping the teacher organize materials, guiding students in understanding instructions, and providing additional support to those who may require it.

During individualized instruction time, the paraprofessional might work with a small group of students to reinforce concepts introduced by the teacher. This requires adaptability to cater to the diverse learning preferences within the group and provide targeted assistance based on individual needs. In the afternoon, the paraprofessional may facilitate a social-emotional learning session where they support students in developing essential life skills.

Throughout the day, the paraprofessional maintains open communication with the teacher, discussing any updates, changes in plans, or specific strategies to address the evolving needs of students. This collaboration ensures a cohesive approach to supporting students' educational and emotional development. By the end of the day, the paraprofessional may reflect on the successes and challenges they encountered. This reflection helps the paraprofessional make adaptations to keep the students learning and growing.

This example illustrates paraprofessionals' dynamic and varied roles and their ability to seamlessly transition between tasks while providing valuable support across different educational experiences. It also showcases the skills needed to embrace the complexity of having different roles and responsibilities on any given day. Being flexible, keeping open lines of communication with other staff, and adopting a servant attitude that you are there to help where needed ensure that you have a successful and purposeful day.

*Flexibility* is defined as "the quality of bending easily without breaking; willingness to change or compromise" (Flexibility, n.d.). There really is no better definition of a paraprofessional: Bend, but don't break. Be willing to adapt and make changes. Be the superhero of flexibility!

## Realistic Expectations

Be willing to adapt and make changes. Be the superhero of flexibility!

As a paraprofessional, you work in a dynamic system with many other people. That means a lot of variables come into play daily. It helps to approach this job with realistic expectations. If today isn't a great day, tomorrow will probably be better.

Begin with morning preparation as you touch base with the teacher and get an idea of what will happen during the day. Then, decide to manage your expectations. You are working with young people, which means things can get messy and unpredictable. If you show up expecting students to manage their behaviors, follow all the rules, say please and thank you, and do exactly what they are told, you are in for a frustrating experience. Keep in mind that elementary students are just beginning to develop self-awareness and self-management skills. They are learning how to express emotions, share space, and follow routines, often for the first time. Middle and high school students are navigating rapid cognitive and emotional changes, including biological challenges with impulse control and emotional regulation. Their brains are still developing the skills needed to pause, reflect, and make sound decisions in the moment. Students are in school to learn all these skills, and you are there to help them learn. By approaching each day knowing there will be some challenges, and accepting that reality, you are heading in the right direction to thrive as a paraprofessional.

## Paraprofessional Requirements

Each state, province, and school district can have different requirements for paraprofessionals. For example, some U.S. states require a high school diploma, while others require two years of college (an associate's degree) and CPR and first aid certifications. Many U.S. states require any adult (aged eighteen or older) who works with students to be fingerprinted, get a background check, and have a tuberculosis test. Once you are hired, you will be asked to fulfill these requirements. With that said, it looks good to have them already fulfilled before you're interviewed and to share that information in your application process.

A paper or online application typically requires you to submit a separate résumé. If you are just starting out and haven't had many job experiences, don't overlook things like babysitting or helping an older adult. Put those experiences on your résumé to show that you like to help and work with others. If you are invited to an interview once your application is processed, prepare yourself to answer interview questions like the following.

- **Question:** "Tell us about yourself and why you are interested in this job."

  When answering, make sure to include that you like to work with children and young people.

  - *Sample answer*—"I've always been passionate about working with children and helping them grow both academically and personally. I have experience volunteering in schools and mentorship programs, and I've found it incredibly rewarding to support students as they gain confidence and new skills. I'm a patient, dependable person who values education and collaboration. I'm especially drawn to this paraprofessional role because it allows me to make a meaningful difference in students' lives while working closely with teachers and other professionals. I'm excited about the opportunity to contribute to a positive and supportive learning environment. "

- **Question:** "What are three adjectives that you would use to describe yourself?"

  Don't be shy! This is your opportunity to brag about yourself.

  - *Sample answer*—"I am compassionate, dependable, and adaptable. I genuinely care about the well-being of students and strive to create a safe and encouraging space for them to learn. I'm dependable and show up every day ready to give my best and be a consistent support in the classroom. I'm adaptable, which is essential in a school setting where things can change quickly. Whether it's shifting plans, addressing student needs, or jumping into a new task, I'm comfortable adjusting and staying focused on what's best for the students."

- **Question:** "How would you handle a situation where a student refused to do their work and had their head on their desk?"

Note that a strong response to this question would emphasize empathy, patience, and relationship building over simple demands for compliance.

* *Sample answer*—"First, I would approach the student quietly and nonconfrontationally to avoid drawing attention to or escalating the situation. I might kneel next to them and say something like 'I noticed you have your head down. Are you feeling OK?' I'd give the student space to respond without pressure. Sometimes, students shut down because they're frustrated, tired, or overwhelmed. If they were open to talking, I'd try to understand the barrier and offer support, whether it was breaking the task into smaller steps, offering a brain break, or just giving them time. My goal would be to preserve the relationship and help the student feel seen and supported, not forced."

Since this is a frequent interview question, let's go into more depth. The best answer might depend on what type of paraprofessional job you are applying for. Here are two additional sample answers for those applying for a specific paraprofessional job related to special education or behavioral intervention.

* *Special education setting sample answer*—"In a special education setting, I would refer to the student's IEP or behavior plan and respond accordingly. If the student has a history of shutting down when overstimulated, I might guide them to a calm space or offer them a sensory tool. I'd use supportive language like 'Let's take a break and come back when you're ready.' I'd also document the behavior and communicate with the teacher or specialist so we could adjust support strategies moving forward."

* *Behavioral support role sample answer*—"As a paraprofessional focused on behavioral intervention, I would see this as an opportunity to reinforce coping strategies we've practiced. I'd try to redirect the student without confrontation, perhaps by offering a preferred activity as a transition back into engagement: 'Would you rather start with a quick drawing and then get to your math?' The goal is to coregulate rather than control. Afterward, I'd check in with the student to reinforce that they can always ask for help or breaks instead of shutting down."

These answers show flexibility, emotional intelligence, and an understanding that as a paraprofessional, you must adapt your approach to the individual needs of each student and the context of your role.

- **Question:** "If someone ran into you at the grocery store and started asking questions about a student in the class you were working in, how would you handle the situation?"

  Remember, confidentiality is critical. (See chapter 3 for more on the importance of confidentiality.)

  - *Sample answer*—"If someone approached me at the grocery store asking questions about a student in my class, I would politely but firmly explain that I'm not able to discuss any student information outside of school. I might say something like 'I'm sorry, I can't talk about students or anything that happens in the classroom. It's important to protect everyone's privacy.' I would then redirect the conversation or excuse myself if needed. Maintaining confidentiality is an important part of my role as a paraprofessional, and I take that responsibility seriously."

By practicing your answers before the interview, you will be prepared to do a great job. Once you get the call that you have been hired, the paperwork and onboarding experience begins.

## The Onboarding Experience

Onboarding experiences for paraprofessionals can vary widely, encompassing a range of activities designed to effectively integrate the paraprofessionals into the school environment. A comprehensive onboarding process might include an initial orientation session that introduces them to school policies, procedures, and expectations. The paraprofessionals might also receive a school tour to become familiar with the facilities and resources available. Shadowing experienced paraprofessionals or teachers can give them practical, hands-on experience and insight into daily responsibilities. Additionally, workshops and training sessions focused on specific skills, such as classroom management, special education techniques, and communication strategies, can equip paraprofessionals with the tools they need to succeed. Regular check-ins with supervisors and mentorship programs can offer paraprofessionals ongoing support and guidance, ensuring they feel confident and prepared. Unfortunately, it is very hard to predict what type of onboarding support you will get as a paraprofessional, and this experience is different in each school district and sometimes at each school site within a district.

Occasionally, paraprofessionals do not receive the level of onboarding they require, and they show up on their first day in need of more direction and clarification about their responsibilities and schedule. If this happens to you, here is some advice on how to handle it: First, take proactive steps to improve your experience. Ask questions. It is easy to think you shouldn't ask too many questions or get in the way since you are new, but how else will you clarify your role and responsibilities? Be brave and initiate discussions with others at the school, such as teachers, office clerks, paraprofessionals, and administrators. Learn more about the school and why you were hired to help. Finding a mentor or buddy can also ensure you get valuable guidance and insight into the school's culture, procedures, and expectations. Keep notes on where your schedule is working well and where there is some confusion so you can clarify this with the teacher during downtime. Finally, let your classroom teacher and school principal or assistant principal know you would appreciate receiving further training and are willing to attend any orientations and workshops. By showing this initiative and eagerness to learn, you are telling the school community that you are there to make a difference.

## Paraprofessional Etiquette

Being a superhero paraprofessional requires attention to the following etiquette items.

- Know your work hours, show up on time, and work the exact hours you are expected to work. Do not come in early or leave late, as you will be paid only for your official hours unless you have an agreement with the administration to work more or less.

- Dress professionally but also appropriately. For example, if you support a student who can scratch others, long-sleeved shirts and pants are called for most days.

- Never talk negatively about the classroom teacher or a student (even if you want to). Maintaining professionalism and trust is essential in your role. If you disagree with the classroom teacher's decision or approach, try to find a way to support it in the moment or respectfully talk with them in private about your concerns. For example, if a teacher chooses a behavior management strategy that you don't think will be effective, you might say afterward, "I noticed [student] was still having a hard time. Would you be open to trying something else we've used before?" Clear, respectful communication helps preserve your working relationship and ensures consistency for the student. However, if you witness something that crosses a professional or ethical line, such as verbal abuse, neglect, or some other action that puts a student's well-being at risk, it's your responsibility to report it. In those rare but serious situations, go directly to a principal or designated school leader. Protecting students is always the top priority.

- Don't use your cell phone unless you are on a break or the teacher asks you to use an app or look something up on your phone. Using your phone during class time can appear unprofessional and may distract you from supervising or supporting students. Staying fully present shows respect for your role and for the learning environment.

- Always be a team player and realize there is a whole school around you. Become part of the school by attending events and being aware of those around you. Your attitude and presence contribute to a positive school culture. Pitching in when needed and showing support across classrooms help you build strong relationships with staff and students alike.

- Keep confidential information confidential at all times. This includes not discussing student behavior, academic performance, or personal matters with friends, family, or even other staff unless that information is relevant to their role. Maintaining trust is essential to protecting students and upholding school policies.

- Ask your lead teacher or the office where you can go when you have a break or downtime. Know where the lounge is, as well as any areas outside where you can sit and relax. Taking your breaks in approved areas ensures that you're easy to locate if you're needed, and it reinforces your role as a responsible professional. These times also give you a chance to recharge so you can return to work refreshed and focused.

- Understand how to report your absences from work. It is impossible to completely avoid illness, and family issues may arise that require you to take a few days off. The earlier you can report an absence, the better it will be for the school, as the school will have more time to find a substitute. Also, know how to request multiple days off if you need to do so. Many districts now use online reporting for absences. Responsibly reporting absences shows that you care about the students and the school and want to make arrangements for coverage as easy on them as possible.

## Meet Chen: Approaching the Day as an Experienced Paraprofessional

Chen has been a paraprofessional at Evergreen Elementary School for over five years. His daily responsibilities include supporting students with special needs, assisting the lead teacher with classroom management, and providing individualized attention to students who require additional help. Here is an example of how Chen approaches his day.

- **Preparing in the morning:** Every day, Chen arrives at school ten minutes before the students. He reviews the day's schedule and lesson plans with the lead teacher, Mrs. Brannam. This routine allows Chen to understand the expectations for the day and prepare any necessary materials or adjustments for the students he supports.

- **Managing expectations:** Chen has learned through experience that every day is different in a school setting. He approaches each day with a flexible mindset, understanding that working in a dynamic system means many variables are at play. Chen knows that while some days may go smoothly, others might be challenging. This realistic perspective helps him remain calm and adaptable.

- **Overcoming daily challenges:** One morning, Chen is assigned to work with a small group of students on a science project. As the class begins, he notices that one of the students, Alex, is having a tough day. Alex, who has autism, is struggling to focus and is becoming increasingly frustrated. Chen recognizes the signs and decides to take a short break with Alex, using a calming strategy they have practiced together. Despite the interruption, Chen remains patient and positive. He understands that Alex's behavior is not a personal insult but a manifestation of his special education challenges. Chen helps Alex reengage with the project by breaking it down into smaller, manageable steps and offering frequent praise and encouragement.

- **Adapting to unpredictability:** Later in the day, during recess, another student, Mia, falls and scrapes her knee. Chen quickly shifts his attention to provide first aid and comfort. He escorts Mia to the nurse and ensures she is cared for before returning to the classroom. These moments of unpredictability are part of Chen's daily routine, and although he would prefer a predictable day, he handles them gracefully and efficiently.

- **Reflecting with a positive outlook:** At the end of the school day, Chen reflects on the day's events with Mrs. Brannam. They discuss what went well and what could be improved for the following day. Chen acknowledges the challenges and celebrates the small victories, like helping Alex complete his project and comforting Mia after her fall. He also shares that he struggled to keep a small reading group on task while he was handling a separate behavioral issue. Together, he and Mrs. Brannam brainstorm ways to manage transitions more smoothly and identify moments when additional support might be needed. Reflecting this way helps Chen feel supported and better prepared for the next day.

Chen's realistic expectations and ability to manage daily challenges allow him to enjoy his role as a paraprofessional. He understands that not every day will be the same, nor will it be perfect, but he finds fulfillment in the progress and growth of the students he supports. His positive attitude and adaptability make him an invaluable school community asset. Chen's case shows how approaching each day with realistic expectations and a flexible mindset can lead to rewarding experiences as a paraprofessional. By accepting the inherent unpredictability of working with children and youth and maintaining focus on their development, paraprofessionals can navigate their role with resilience and compassion while contributing to a positive learning environment.

## Wrap-Up

This chapter launched your journey of professional growth and transformation into a superhero paraprofessional by discussing the importance of this incredible job, the different paraprofessional roles, the requirements to become a paraprofessional, and important professional etiquette to remember while working as a paraprofessional. In the feature box that follows, you'll find practical advice from experienced paraprofessionals. Their insights are grounded in day-to-day experience. Then, in the "Notes and Reflections: Being a Superhero Paraprofessional" reproducible (page 22), you'll have the opportunity to thoughtfully reflect on what you've learned and consider how these insights apply to your own practice. These moments of reflection are an essential part of your ongoing learning as you prepare to explore the next chapter on developing a strong paraprofessional mindset.

## *Advice from*
### SUPERHERO PARAPROFESSIONALS

"First and foremost, communication is key. Make it a habit to touch base with your teachers regularly. Clear communication helps clarify expectations and ensures we're all on the same page. Don't be shy—ask questions! If there's any uncertainty about your responsibilities, seek clarification."

(E. Gomez, personal communication, May 30, 2024)

"Don't hesitate to initiate meetings. Schedule regular check-ins with teachers or team members to discuss your role, address any uncertainties, and collaborate on effective ways to contribute to the classroom. It's all about open communication!"

(N. Berry, personal communication, June 15, 2024)

"When I enter the classroom every weekday, it is with the mindset that my job is in a supporting role. I want to do everything I can to help the teacher accomplish her goals for the day."

(B. O'Brien, personal communication, November 8, 2024)

# Notes and Reflections: Being a Superhero Paraprofessional

Take a few moments to reflect on the following questions about being a superhero paraprofessional.

1. What aspects of being a paraprofessional do you find most appealing, and why?

2. Is there a specific type of paraprofessional role that interests you the most? Why?

3. How do you see yourself making an impact on a student's life in this role?

4. What proactive steps could you take if you experienced a weak onboarding process at a new school?

5. How do you think that working as a paraprofessional will challenge you to grow personally and professionally?

# Developing a Paraprofessional Mindset

**2**

Have you ever wondered what separates a good paraprofessional from a great paraprofessional—or a superhero paraprofessional? The answer might surprise you. It's not about superhuman strength or the ability to fly (although boundless energy certainly helps). It all boils down to a strong set of skills that empower you to make a real difference in the lives of your students. This chapter explores those skills, beginning with the ten traits of outstanding paraprofessionals. Then, you'll learn about the power of an asset-based pedagogy and a growth mindset. So, grab your cape and get ready to unleash your inner superhero!

## Ten Traits of Outstanding Paraprofessionals

Outstanding paraprofessionals bring a powerful combination of heart, skill, and professionalism to the classroom. These individuals not only support instruction but also help create a positive,

### KEY POINTS

- Learn about the characteristics of superhero paraprofessionals.
- Go from an excellent paraprofessional to a superhero paraprofessional.
- Become more proactive and collaborative.
- Embrace a growth mindset.
- Stretch beyond your comfort zone and collaborate with others.

productive, and inclusive learning environment. The following ten traits represent the foundation of excellence in this role. Whether you're just starting your journey or continuing to grow in your career, developing these traits will help you make a lasting impact on your students and your school community.

### Trait 1: Organized—The Master of Schedules and Supplies

Imagine a classroom running like a well-oiled machine: Students are learning, materials are readily available, and lesson plans flow seamlessly. That's the power of organizational skills! As a paraprofessional, you'll be a master of tasks, keeping track of student schedules, managing learning materials, and ensuring student progress is documented. Mastering organization allows you to anticipate needs, stay on top of deadlines, and contribute to a calm and focused learning environment. Even if organization is not your strength, it is something you can learn. Following are some of the most important tasks for organization.

- Create daily checklists of the most important items that students need to accomplish.

- Prepare materials ahead of time.

- Use color-coding systems (for example, different-colored folders or labels) for various students or groups to keep paperwork and assignments easy to locate.

- Use timers or phone alarms to keep track of transitions.

- Set a routine for doing and a location for storing documentation and paperwork.

- Regularly declutter your work area, as well as student spaces you support, to minimize distractions.

- Use well-organized teachers as resources and as models to strengthen your skills.

The first step to improving your organizational skills is to become aware of different ways that you can keep organized.

### Trait 2: Positive—A Daily Dose of Sunshine

Let's face it—as with any profession, some days on the job will be challenging. In the classroom, a positive attitude is your secret weapon. By approaching each day enthusiastically and believing in each student's potential, you create a ripple effect of optimism. Your positive energy is contagious, motivating students to learn and persevere through difficulties. Remember, a smile and a can-do spirit can make all the difference, even on tough days. Here are some ways you can keep your outlook bright.

- Start your day with gratitude and reflect on the positive aspects of your job and the people you work with.

- Focus on using positive language and celebrating the small wins that each student accomplishes.

- Find other positive people to be around at work, and avoid those who complain and want to dampen your spirit.

- End your day by reflecting on at least one good thing that happened during the day, and prepare for another positive day tomorrow.

### Trait 3: Professional—The Standard for Excellence

Professionalism is the foundation of trust and respect. It is about showing up on time and dressing for the job, but it also means being committed to your role in more substantial ways. You are a role model for students, and your professionalism demonstrates the importance of taking pride in your work. How can you model professionalism?

- Be reliable. Arrive on time, be prepared, and follow through on responsibilities.

- Show a strong work ethic and be willing to go the extra mile to help students, teachers, and fellow staff.

- Always maintain confidentiality. Avoid gossip, and if a colleague is sharing confidential information inappropriately, redirect the conversation or report the concern to your classroom teacher.

- Communicate professionally by using respectful language, maintaining a calm tone, listening actively, and avoiding slang or sarcasm in work conversations.

- Take initiative by seeking feedback. Ask your classroom teacher, specialists, or veteran paraprofessionals for suggestions on how you can improve your support. You might also invite informal feedback by asking the classroom teacher, "Is there anything I could do differently next time to be more helpful?"

*Trait 4: Collaborative—A Builder of Bridges, Not Walls*

Collaboration is critical in the job of a paraprofessional. You'll be working alongside teachers, administrators, other paraprofessionals, and, of course, students. How can you be a strong team player?

- **Be an active listener:** This means giving others your full attention when they speak, making eye contact, nodding, paraphrasing their message to show understanding, and avoiding interrupting them. Active listening shows respect and helps build trust.

- **Communicate clearly and respectfully with coworkers:** Speak with kindness and professionalism, even when discussing difficult topics. Always use calm tones, thoughtful wording, and a problem-solving mindset.

- **Share ideas:** Your daily work with students gives you valuable insights. For example, you might notice that a student responds well to visual cues or hands-on tasks; sharing that observation with the teacher could inform future lessons. You can also suggest strategies you've successfully used in previous roles or ask to help adapt activities for different learners.

- **Be open to compromise and willing to defer to the teacher's judgment:** There may be times when you disagree with the teacher's approach. For example, you may feel that a student needs a break during a lesson, but the teacher chooses to redirect the student's behavior instead. In these situations, it's important to support the teacher's decision and follow through with their plan. Afterward, you can respectfully discuss your observations and offer ideas for future adjustments.

- **Offer support to team members in need of assistance:** If another paraprofessional is overwhelmed or a teacher is managing multiple needs at once, offer a helping hand. Small acts of teamwork go a long way.

As a paraprofessional, you play a vital role in supporting teachers and the overall teaching team to ensure that all students receive the best possible learning experience. Your unique perspective, gained through daily interactions with students, allows you to offer important insights about how students are engaging with lessons, where they may be struggling, and how their individual needs can be better supported.

- Be aware that every team is different and that you will need to adapt to the unique team you are working with.

- Respect your teammates if they have a different perspective than you, and seek to understand where they are coming from.

- As you work with your team, stay focused on the goal of student achievement and well-being, as that will ground your work in what is most important.

- Last, celebrate the small and large successes of your team. Teamwork makes the dream come true!

### Trait 5: Knowledgeable About Instruction—More Than Just a Helping Hand

While you might not be the lead teacher, understanding instructional strategies and techniques is a superpower for paraprofessionals. You learn these strategies by becoming a student of the job. Knowing different learning preferences and how to implement effective strategies empowers you to better support students. This knowledge allows you to tailor your approach to individual needs so that you make learning more engaging and accessible for everyone. The more tools you have at your disposal, the easier your job will be. Outstanding paraprofessionals do the following things to increase their available tools.

- Observe and learn from teachers daily, taking notes to refer to at a later date. Pay attention to how the teachers introduce new concepts, manage transitions, and interact with students; these small observations can become powerful tools in your own practice.

- Seek out online resources like websites, blogs, and video platforms that provide tutorials on instructional methods and teaching strategies.

  - **Edutopia (www.edutopia.org):** This website features practical articles and videos on classroom strategies, student engagement, and inclusive practices.

  - **IRIS Center (https://iris.peabody.vanderbilt.edu):** This website offers free online modules on topics like behavior management, differentiated instruction, and support of students with disabilities.

  - **Pocketful of Primary (www.youtube.com/@PocketfulofPrimary):** This channel offers clear, engaging classroom routines and instructional techniques, often with real classroom footage.

  - **Understood (www.understood.org):** This website focuses on helping educators support students with learning and thinking differences. It is especially useful for working with diverse learners.

- Take advantage of school- or district-sponsored trainings. These sessions are often designed to support your specific role and can introduce new tools or strategies that will enhance your day-to-day work.

- Seek out other paraprofessionals to exchange ideas on working with different students. Collaborating with peers can spark creative solutions and help you feel more supported and connected in your work.

- Build a resource library with books, articles, and materials on instructional strategies and techniques, which you can refer to at a moment's notice. Having trusted go-to resources lets you adapt quickly when student needs shift or new challenges arise.

### Trait 6: Communicative—The Art of Making Connections

Clear, effective communication is vital for building positive relationships with students, teachers, and other staff members. How you talk to a student differs from how you talk to the office manager, and talking to one teacher may require different communication skills than talking to another. Becoming a strong communicator allows you to effectively share information, address concerns, celebrate student achievements, and adapt your communication style to different audiences. Strong communicators do the following.

- They become expert active listeners who focus on listening rather than just waiting to speak.

- They maintain eye contact and give their full attention to the speaker.

- They use positive body language, nod to show engagement, and make facial expressions to match what is being communicated.

- They ask follow-up questions for clarification.

- They keep communication channels open with teachers and fellow staff members, whether about student progress or daily tasks, to strengthen the team and better serve students.

### Trait 7: Adaptable—The Master of Change

The classroom is dynamic; things sometimes go differently than planned. That's where adaptability comes in. This adaptability allows you to adjust your strategies quickly, whether it's for a sudden change in the lesson plan or a student who needs additional support. The sooner you accept and embrace that no two days will be alike, the more effective you will be. By embracing change and thinking on your feet, you can ensure a smooth learning experience for everyone. Paraprofessionals who have mastered being adaptable do the following.

- They remain calm under pressure and maintain a composed demeanor that helps students stay focused; this encourages a positive atmosphere even in challenging situations.

- They are flexible and able to prioritize tasks to stay focused on what is most important. They assess what needs immediate attention and what can be addressed later.

- They collaborate with other staff members to participate in team decision making.

- They have backup plans ready, which include different activities and strategies to keep learning going strong when there is an unanticipated shift.

### Trait 8: Constantly Learning—The Never-Ending Quest for Knowledge

The world of education is constantly changing and evolving, which means the most effective paraprofessionals are lifelong learners. By seeking new knowledge and professional development opportunities, you stay up-to-date on best practices and refine your skills. Learning doesn't stop when we finish school; it's a continuous journey that fuels growth and enhances our ability to support students. Some topics you may want to explore include instructional strategies, ways of working with challenging students, and techniques to use with special needs students. Paraprofessionals who are lifelong learners do the following.

- They set personal learning goals about specific topics to learn more about.

- They attend workshops and trainings when those are offered, and they access online videos and learning opportunities to target specific areas of working with students.

- They keep up with new research and trends in books and articles to enhance their practice.

- They maintain curiosity by asking questions to gain a deeper understanding for growth.

### Trait 9: Respectful of Diversity—Celebration of Our Differences

Every classroom is a tapestry of students with diverse backgrounds, experiences, and learning preferences. A strong paraprofessional values and respects these differences. You can contribute to a welcoming and inclusive environment by celebrating diversity and fostering a sense of belonging for all students. Paraprofessionals who respect diversity do the following.

- They explore their own cultural background, beliefs, and ideas first because awareness of oneself makes it easier to recognize that everyone has a unique story and background deserving of respect and celebration.

- They educate themselves about cultural awareness and learn about the traditions and backgrounds of students.

- They work with the teacher to create an inclusive classroom environment where all students feel represented and valued. They do this by displaying diverse books, artwork, and materials, as well as integrating culturally relevant content into lessons to reflect the richness of their students' backgrounds.

- They always model respectful behavior and language.

### Trait 10: Patient and Empathetic—Someone Who Walks in Students' Shoes

Building strong relationships with students requires patience and empathy. These qualities allow you to connect more deeply with students, understand their challenges, and offer support and encouragement. By showing genuine interest in the students and what they enjoy doing and learning about, you exhibit respect to them, and they can sense that respect and usually reciprocate it. By demonstrating patience and empathy, you create a safe space for students to learn and grow, which fosters a sense of trust. Paraprofessionals who are patient and empathetic do the following.

- They recognize that each student is unique and take the time to learn about their strengths, challenges, and preferences. This makes it easier to respond calmly when they need to adapt and practice empathy and compassion because students are having a tough time.

- They communicate understanding about student challenges and say that it's OK to struggle sometimes; this shows care that builds trust.

- They give students space when they need time to regroup, and they welcome them back to learning when they are ready.

These top ten traits for paraprofessionals are essential building blocks to help you contribute to a supportive and inclusive learning environment. When paraprofessionals consistently show up with these traits, they send a powerful message to students: "You are seen, valued, and capable." This message lays the foundation for deeper instructional practices like asset-based pedagogy, which takes that belief a step further by intentionally recognizing and building on each student's strengths and lived experiences.

## Asset-Based Pedagogy

Asset-based pedagogy is an educational approach that focuses on students' assets—their strengths and abilities. This perspective emphasizes the value of students' cultural, linguistic, and personal experiences, and it uses these as a foundation for learning. In contrast to deficit-based models, which highlight what students lack, asset-based pedagogy helps educators celebrate diversity, see students as capable learners, and work to create an environment where all students can thrive. By shifting the focus to students' potential and resources, this approach promotes a more inclusive and equitable classroom environment.

As you work with many different students, you will quickly realize that all students have strengths as well as strong areas of interest. One student might struggle with reading but be able to draw incredible pictures and diagrams. Another might find mathematics very challenging but have incredible talent as a young leader in group work. By starting where the student is strong and recognizing the many assets they enter the classroom with, you can use those strengths to gain momentum in a lot of other areas. Research shows a strength-based approach has a powerful impact (Paterson, 2022); it shifts the focus from filling in learning gaps to identifying what students already know and can do and building on that knowledge. Building on their strengths allows students to experience successes and "wins" in their learning, leading to more motivation and success (Paterson, 2022).

The following are some practical ways you can begin to implement asset-based instructional routines and strategies with students (Fink, 2023). As a paraprofessional, you may not design the curriculum, but you play a vital role in supporting its delivery and reinforcing these practices in everyday student interactions. Through your close relationships with students and your role in small-group and one-on-one support, you are uniquely positioned to apply asset-based strategies in meaningful, hands-on ways.

- **Recognize and value students' backgrounds:** Start by learning about your students' cultures, languages, and life experiences. Show interest in their backgrounds by asking them about their interests, family traditions, and personal experiences. This helps you understand the wealth of knowledge they bring to the classroom and lets students feel seen and heard. For example, you can integrate discussions or projects where students share aspects of their cultural heritages, traditions, or interests, especially during small-group time or in casual classroom conversations.

- **Use culturally relevant curriculum:** While you may not be responsible for selecting curriculum materials, you can help students engage more deeply by drawing connections between the lesson and their lived experiences. Use texts, media, or vocabulary words that reflect their interests or cultural backgrounds. For instance, when helping a student read a passage or complete an assignment, consider highlighting examples that resonate with their community or history, or asking questions that invite personal connections.

- **Encourage student voice and agency:** Empower students by giving them opportunities to share their ideas, opinions, and perspectives, even in everyday interactions. You might ask a student how they would solve a problem, ask them what they think about a story you're reading together, or let them choose between tasks when appropriate. These small but intentional choices build engagement and show students that their thinking matters.

- **Create collaborative learning environments:** Support classroom activities that involve students working together in pairs or small groups. You can model respectful collaboration, guide conversations, and encourage students to recognize and appreciate their peers' strengths. Whether you are facilitating a peer discussion or supporting a partner activity, your role in promoting teamwork directly supports the inclusive values of asset-based pedagogy.

- **Focus on growth, not deficits:** When providing feedback, be specific about what students are doing well and where they can improve. You can frame challenges as opportunities for growth rather than as weaknesses. Praise effort, persistence, and progress. For example, instead of simply pointing out mistakes, provide constructive feedback that helps students build on what they already know; use language that highlights their potential to overcome challenges.

Another powerful piece that fits into this asset-based approach is the expectations that we hold for our students. Research has proven that our expectations of what students can actually do and learn have a direct relationship with student achievement (Hattie, 2023). The research is clear that high expectations—expecting your students to achieve at high levels, use their strengths, and reach their goals—are directly linked to higher student achievement and success. By embracing student assets and keeping your expectations high, you can help foster an atmosphere where students feel valued, capable, and motivated to succeed. Working with students with this view that they have many different strengths and abilities will help you celebrate what students do well as you help them with the areas where they struggle. It is very empowering for students to learn that there are more than one or two ways to show how smart they are. Now that is superhero stuff!

Holding high expectations for students and celebrating the many individual assets that each student has are just part of the bigger picture—how we, the adults, *think* about learning and growth and how our thoughts play a critical role in student success. That's where mindset comes in. Just as we believe in our students' potential to grow, we must also adopt that same belief for ourselves. The attitude we bring into the classroom, especially when things get hard, can either open the door to new possibilities or reinforce limitations. To continue building on the asset-based approach, we need to understand how cultivating a growth mindset can transform the way we work, learn, and support others.

## A Growth Mindset: The Power of *Yet*

Having a growth mindset as a paraprofessional is essential for fostering both personal and professional development. This mindset, which emphasizes the belief that abilities and intelligence can be developed through dedication and hard work, allows us to embrace challenges, persist in the face of setbacks, and continuously seek learning opportunities (Dweck, 2006, 2017). By adopting a growth mindset, you can view feedback and constructive criticism as valuable tools for improvement rather than judgments on your abilities. This perspective sets a positive example for the students you support, encouraging them to approach their own learning with resilience and optimism (Dweck, 2006, 2017). Ultimately, a growth mindset enables you to adapt to the educational environment's ever-changing demands and better meet your students' diverse needs.

A growth mindset will enable you to view challenges not as obstacles but as opportunities for growth. By approaching your work with this perspective, you can develop new competencies, enhance your existing skills, and better support the students and educators you serve as a paraprofessional. You may learn to say, "I am not as strong as I would like to be in this area *yet*." By adding that *yet* to the end of the statement, you are telling yourself that you will eventually get there and learn the skills you need. Cultivating this growth mindset and embracing the power of *yet* can profoundly impact your professional trajectory. It encourages you to seek learning opportunities, experiment with new approaches, and learn from mistakes. This mindset fosters a sense of resilience and self-efficacy, empowering you to take on increasingly complex tasks and responsibilities. It also reminds you to accept and embrace imperfection. None of us are perfect, and we are all on a journey of learning and becoming (Dweck, 2006, 2017).

A growth mindset is a superpower for any paraprofessional. It allows you to see challenges as opportunities to learn and progress for yourself and the students you support. It fuels your creativity in finding new strategies and adapting to different learning preferences. With a growth mindset, you celebrate small victories as stepping stones to more significant achievements and nurture perseverance. A can-do attitude goes a long way!

> By adding that *yet* to the end of the statement, you are telling yourself that you will eventually get there and learn the skills you need.

Many well-meaning paraprofessionals do fantastic work and care deeply for their students. However, some go beyond and become true superheroes who make a profound impact on their students, colleagues, and school community. What sets these individuals apart? Let's explore the work life of Tyler, our case study paraprofessional.

## Meet Tyler: Developing From a Good to a Great Paraprofessional

Tyler has been a paraprofessional at Daily School for three years, primarily working with students with severe behavioral challenges. Because he is dedicated to his role, he has always sought to improve his skills. In his third year, Tyler's principal, Mr. Nolan, has recognized his remarkable growth, noting that Tyler transitioned from a good paraprofessional to a superhero paraprofessional. What changed? Let's break down the two-year journey that led to this success.

Tyler's first-year approach to his role was grounded in passion and dedication. However, there were areas for improvement.

- **He used reactionary behavior management:** Tyler tackled behavioral incidents as they happened. He used familiar techniques but often felt like he was playing the carnival game *Whac-A-Mole* with challenges constantly popping up in every direction.

- **His student connections were underdeveloped:** Tyler worked hard to form bonds with students, which helped establish trust, but he often struggled to fully understand the root causes of student behavior.

- **He was hesitant to seek support:** Tyler avoided asking the classroom teacher or other staff for guidance because he didn't want to burden them with concerns or unwanted questions.

While Tyler was doing well, his approach remained reactive rather than proactive. His student connections were not as strong as they could be, and he was hesitant to seek support, which limited the long-term impact he could have on students' success.

In his second year, Tyler's transformation was driven by a shift toward proactive, strategic interventions and a deeper understanding of his students' needs.

- **He mastered proactive intervention:** Tyler learned to recognize early warning signs of escalating behavior and applied de-escalation strategies before situations became crises. This led to the creation of a calmer classroom environment.

- **He understood students on a deeper level:** Tyler took time to learn about his students' backgrounds, triggers, and learning preferences. This enabled him to tailor his support and address core behavioral challenges more effectively.

- **He collaborated with teachers:** Instead of working in isolation, Tyler shared insights about proactive behavior strategies and positive reinforcement with the classroom teacher. The teacher saw significant improvements and decided to implement some of Tyler's techniques with all students.

- **He expanded his impact:** When his assigned students were showing remarkable progress, Tyler had more capacity to assist other students in the classroom and extend his influence beyond just a few individuals.

- **He became a resource for the school:** As word spread about Tyler's success, teachers sought his expertise. They invited him to share his strategies during collaborative meetings, where he helped elevate the entire school's approach to behavior management.

Tyler's transformation into a superhero paraprofessional is just the beginning. Now more excited than ever, he is committed to refining his skills, collaborating with colleagues, and ensuring every student receives the proactive, personalized support they need to thrive. By shifting from reactive management to proactive engagement, Tyler has proven that superhero paraprofessionals don't just support students—they empower them to succeed.

## Wrap-Up

This chapter discussed the top ten traits of successful paraprofessionals and the importance of using an asset-based approach with students and having a growth mindset for ourselves. In the feature box that follows, you'll find practical advice from experienced paraprofessionals. Their insights are grounded in day-to-day experience. Then, in the "Notes and Reflections: Rising to the Challenge—Developing a Paraprofessional Mindset" reproducible (page 38), you'll have the opportunity to thoughtfully reflect on what you've learned and consider how these insights apply to your own practice. Prioritize the time you spend in reflection, as this is a powerful way to continue growing as a paraprofessional.

# *Advice From*
## SUPERHERO PARAPROFESSIONALS

"It is important for educational paraprofessionals to proactively address any issues that may arise among students. This includes conflicts, bullying, or other negative behaviors that can impact peer relationships. Don't just wait for the teacher or another adult to address issues. Jump on in and show initiative and be proactive."

(G. Nelson, personal communication, September 20, 2024)

"Once I accepted that no two days were going to be the same, I started to enjoy the variety of the job. I have only had office jobs that were basically the same every day, so it took a while to learn that variety is not a bad thing and keeps me on my toes."

(K. Tran, personal communication, June 30, 2024)

"I like to stay informed about best practices in education. As an educational paraprofessional, I try to attend professional development workshops and conferences to learn new strategies and techniques for supporting students. There are also more online resources to learn from."

(Y. Poster, personal communication, July 22, 2024)

# Notes and Reflections: Rising to the Challenge—Developing a Paraprofessional Mindset

Take a few moments to reflect on the following questions about being a superhero paraprofessional.

1. What are your biggest strengths and areas for growth based on the ten superhero traits shared in this chapter?

2. How can looking for students' assets help you become a superhero paraprofessional?

3. How can recognizing a student's strengths positively impact their motivation and engagement in learning?

4. How can you use the power of *yet* to grow professionally and personally?

5. Are there specific areas where you'd like to learn more to enhance your skills?

# 3

# Supporting Students With Special Needs

Many paraprofessionals work with students who have special needs. You may encounter a wide range of disabilities in this position, and knowledge is a superpower. Like a superhero, you step in with patience, adaptability, and unwavering support, helping students navigate challenges and achieve their full potential. Every day brings new opportunities to make a difference, proving that the real heroes in special education don't wear capes—they walk the halls and offer guidance, encouragement, and the belief that every student can succeed.

This chapter addresses special education laws and regulations; special education disabilities; individual education programs; the continuums of special education student and paraprofessional placement; the importance of confidentiality; supporting students with medical concerns and autism spectrum disorder; and addressing communication barriers for students with speech and language impairments.

## KEY POINTS

- Understand the requirements for a paraprofessional who works with students with special needs.

- Learn about the laws surrounding special education, what an Individualized Education Program (IEP) is, and why an IEP is important.

- Explore the different types of special needs and disabilities that a paraprofessional may support in the classroom.

- Learn about the continuum of services for special needs students and how that relates to different types of paraprofessional jobs and compensation.

## Understanding Special Education Laws and Regulations

Special education programs are based on federal and state (or provincial) laws that provide regulations for all educators who work with students with special needs. One of the most important laws governing special education in the United States is the Individuals With Disabilities Education Act (IDEA, 2004). This federal law mandates that all students with disabilities are entitled to a free and appropriate public education in the least restrictive environment. It also outlines the process for developing Individualized Education Programs for students with disabilities, which spell out the goals, accommodations, and services students will receive at school. In addition to IDEA, state laws and regulations govern special education in each state. These laws need to meet the regulations from IDEA yet can vary from state to state. For example, states may differ in the eligibility categories for special education or use different terms for specific disabilities. Some states differ in how many days are required to complete a special education assessment. It is the special education teacher's and administrator's responsibility to make sure the laws and regulations are being followed at all times and to ensure that your work is in line with those laws. Take time to ask the specialists at your school about any regulations you need to be aware of in your work.

Paraprofessionals working in special education should also be aware of the Americans With Disabilities Act (1990), a federal law that prohibits discrimination based on disability in all aspects of public life, including education. The foundation of this law ensures that students with disabilities have equal access to educational opportunities and facilities. It also protects the rights of students with disabilities to receive accommodations and modifications to help them succeed in school. What is important for you to know is that all students have a right to a free and appropriate education, no matter how severe their disabilities are, and you play a critical role in helping them access that.

## Understanding Special Education Disabilities

Students with special needs represent a broad range of disabilities. What follows are some of the most common disabilities that make students eligible for special education services (Schaeffer, 2023). Note that it's good for paraprofessionals to get used to the many acronyms that represent these disabilities, as they will often show up on any number of forms and documents.

### Learning Disability

A learning disability (LD) is a neurological condition that affects how a person processes information. It reflects the brain's way of interpreting and using information, not the person's intelligence. Students with a learning disability may struggle with reading (dyslexia), writing (dysgraphia), mathematics (dyscalculia), or language processing. These difficulties can impact their academic performance and self-esteem. With appropriate interventions, accommodations, and instructional strategies, students with a learning disability can succeed in school and beyond. You can learn more by visiting the National Center for Learning Disabilities' website (https://ncld.org).

### Autism Spectrum Disorder

Autism spectrum disorder (ASD) is a developmental disorder that affects communication, social interaction, and behavior. The term *spectrum* refers to the wide range of abilities and challenges that individuals with autism spectrum disorder may experience. Some students may have difficulty understanding social cues, maintaining eye contact, or engaging in conversations, while others may struggle with sensory sensitivities or repetitive behaviors. Students with autism spectrum disorder may need structured routines, visual supports, and individualized approaches to learning and social interaction. To learn more about autism, you can visit the following organizations' websites: Autism Speaks (www.autismspeaks.org) and the Autistic Self Advocacy Network (https://autisticadvocacy.org).

### Intellectual Disability

Students with an intellectual disability (ID) have significant limitations in cognitive functioning, reasoning, problem solving, and adaptive behavior, which include daily life skills such as communication, self-care, and social interaction. These students typically require a highly individualized learning environment, often in a self-contained classroom, where they focus on both academic skills and life skills that promote independence. Intellectual disabilities can range from mild to profound, and students may require ongoing support into adulthood. Visit the following organizations' websites to learn more: the Arc (https://thearc.org) and the American Association on Intellectual and Developmental Disabilities (www.aaidd.org).

### Speech or Language Impairment

Speech or language impairment (SLI) can impact students' ability to understand, process, and express spoken language. These impairments may include difficulties with articulation (pronouncing words correctly), fluency (speaking without stuttering), receptive language (understanding spoken information), or expressive language (effectively communicating thoughts and ideas). Many students with speech or language impairments receive support from a speech-language pathologist through pull-out services or push-in therapy within the classroom. To learn more, visit the American Speech-Language-Hearing Association's website (www.asha.org/public).

### Hearing Impairment

Hearing impairment (HI) can range from mild hearing loss to complete deafness. Students with hearing loss may struggle with speech development, language comprehension, and communication. They may use hearing aids, cochlear implants, or other assistive technologies. Some students rely on sign language or lip reading, and they may need accommodations like captioned materials, speech-to-text technology, or an interpreter in the classroom. To learn more, visit the websites of the National Association of the Deaf (www.nad.org) and the Hearing Loss Association of America (www.hearingloss.org).

### Visual Impairment

Visual impairment (VI), ranging from partial vision loss to total blindness, affects a student's ability to access information through sight. Students with visual impairments may require specialized instructional materials, such as braille, large-print, or audio-based resources. Orientation and mobility training, along with assistive technology like screen readers, can help these students navigate both academic and real-world environments. Learn more about visual impairments by visiting the websites of the American Foundation for the Blind (www.afb.org) and the National Federation of the Blind (https://nfb.org).

### Emotional Disturbance

Emotional disturbance (ED) refers to significant challenges in regulating emotions and behaviors that impact a student's ability to learn and interact with others. This may include anxiety disorders, depression, mood disorders, or difficulty managing anger. Students with emotional disturbance may struggle with relationships, exhibit unpredictable behaviors, or have difficulty coping with school demands. They often benefit from structured routines, social-emotional learning supports, counseling, and behavioral intervention plans. To learn more, visit the websites of the Child Mind Institute (https://childmind.org) and Mental Health America (https://mhanational.org).

### Other Health Impairments

The other health impairment (OHI) category encompasses a broad range of medical conditions that can affect a student's stamina, strength, or alertness in the classroom. This includes attention deficit hyperactivity disorder (ADHD), chronic illnesses (such as epilepsy, diabetes, or asthma), neurological conditions (such as Tourette's syndrome), and physical disabilities (such as cerebral palsy). Traumatic brain injuries may also fall under this category, as they can affect cognition, memory, or physical functioning. Students with OHI often require accommodations such as modified schedules, medical supports, or physical therapy to help them succeed in school. Here are some organizations that provide further information on specific disabilities.

- Children and Adults with Attention-Deficit/Hyperactivity Disorder (CHADD; https://chadd.org)
- Epilepsy Foundation (www.epilepsy.com)
- Tourette Association of America (https://tourette.org)
- Brain Injury Association of America (https://biausa.org)

Understanding the wide range of disabilities that students may experience is an important first step in supporting them effectively. Each student's needs, abilities, and learning profile are unique, and addressing those differences requires more than just awareness—it requires a structured plan. That's where the Individualized Education Program (IEP) comes in. As a paraprofessional, you will play a key role in helping implement the goals and accommodations outlined in a student's IEP, even if you are not directly involved in writing it. The next section will guide you through what an IEP is, how it is developed, and how you can support students in meeting their individualized goals.

## Understanding Individualized Education Programs

Students with disabilities will each have an IEP, a legally binding document designed to outline the education program and goals that the student needs to aim to reach. IEPs are created through a collaborative process involving parents, teachers, school staff, and often specialists. They are tailored to meet the unique needs of the student. Each U.S. state outlines what is included in an IEP document in that state.

Asking to see a student's IEP or talking with the special education teacher about the IEP is a great place to start to become knowledgeable about the student's program. Some teachers will provide their paraprofessionals with access to the IEP and ask that they read through it themselves. Other teachers will summarize the IEP for paraprofessionals. If the teacher you work with doesn't mention a student's IEP, show initiative by asking about it to clarify the goals the student is working toward.

### What an IEP Looks Like

An IEP is a multipage document that contains a lot of important information about the student. The first page usually contains important information about the student, including their full name, birthday, grade, and parents' names. Most IEPs will then specify the following.

- **Goals:** Measurable goals that help determine whether a student is making progress and whether the program is effective

- **Accommodations:** Modifications that help the student participate in school activities and achieve their IEP goals

- **Least restrictive environment:** A guiding principle that ensures students with IEPs are educated with their nondisabled peers to the maximum extent possible

- **Progress measurements:** A description of how the student's progress will be measured and reported to their parents

- **Current level of performance:** An assessment of the student's starting point with assessment and testing information

- **Service delivery:** A plan for how the student will achieve their goals

To see a sample IEP, visit the National Association of Special Education Teachers' website (www.naset.org).

### IEP at a Glance

When working with a student with an IEP, educators might find it useful to develop an IEP at a Glance document. This is a tool that summarizes key components of a student's IEP in just one or two pages but still includes all the pertinent information that you and other specialists need to know when working with the student. It should be clear, concise, and easily accessible for all team members.

Here's the information that is typically included in an IEP at a Glance document.

- **Student information:** Full name, date of birth, grade level, and school year

- **Disability category:** The specific disability or disabilities that the student has been diagnosed with

- **Goals and objectives:** Short-term objectives and annual goals for the student (both academic and functional) and how progress will be measured

- **Accommodations and modifications:** Specific accommodations to help the student access the curriculum (such as extended test time and preferential seating) and modifications (like changes to the content or performance expectations)

- **Services and supports:** A description of the services the student will receive (for example, speech therapy or occupational therapy) and the frequency, duration, and location of these services

- **Behavioral interventions and supports:** Any behavior-related goals or strategies in place to support positive behavior, and specific behavioral intervention plans if applicable

- **Service delivery model:** A description of how services are provided (pull-out services, inclusion settings, or one-on-one support)

This condensed overview of the longer IEP document's most important information is easier to read and comprehend. Figure 3.1 (page 46) shows a sample IEP at a Glance document, but this is just one example; an at-a-glance page can be set up in many different ways. Ask the teacher you are working with if they have a summary view of a student's IEP. If not, you can always use the previous list or the following sample document to guide your information-gathering efforts.

### Paraprofessional Support Within the IEP

As a superhero paraprofessional, your role is essential in ensuring that students with disabilities receive the services and accommodations outlined in their IEPs. The IEP is a legal document that outlines a student's educational goals, services, and accommodations, and your support helps turn those plans into reality. Here's how you will play a critical role in a student's educational journey.

- **Supporting classroom activities:** Your role in the classroom goes beyond simply assisting students; you are actively helping them access

# IEP at a Glance

Student Name: _____  Grade: _____

Eligibility: _____  Annual IEP Date: _____

| Goal Areas | Accommodations |
|---|---|
| | |

| Service | Days | Time per Week or Day |
|---|---|---|
| | | |
| | | |
| | | |
| | | |

| Goals |
|---|
| |

**Figure 3.1: IEP at a Glance tool.**

the curriculum. This might include modifying assignments, using visual aids, breaking tasks into smaller steps, or providing one-on-one or small-group instruction. Since each student's needs are unique, the strategies you use will be guided by students' IEP accommodations to ensure the students receive the necessary support to succeed alongside their peers.

- **Providing behavioral support:** Many students with disabilities have behavioral intervention plans as part of their IEPs. As a paraprofessional, you may help implement these plans by using positive reinforcement, structured routines, and redirection techniques. Collecting data on behaviors—such as frequency, duration, and triggers—helps the team assess whether current strategies are effective or need adjustment. Your consistency in following the behavioral intervention plan can make a significant impact on a student's ability to self-regulate and engage in learning.

- **Monitoring progress:** Paraprofessionals play a key role in tracking and documenting students' progress toward their IEP goals. The special education teacher will provide guidance on what data to collect and how to document it. Whether it's academic achievement, behavioral improvement, or skill development, this information is crucial for IEP meetings, as it helps determine whether interventions are working or if adjustments are needed. Your observations and records directly contribute to shaping a student's future support plan.

- **Promoting social and emotional development:** Many students with disabilities struggle with social interactions, communication, and emotional regulation. Your role may involve encouraging peer interactions, helping students practice social skills, and guiding them through difficult moments. For example, you might support a student in taking turns during group work, using appropriate language in conversations, or managing frustration in a productive way. These skills are just as vital as academic success and can significantly improve a student's confidence and ability to connect with others.

- **Implementing specific therapies:** For students receiving specialized therapies, such as speech-language or occupational therapy, your support can extend beyond the therapy session. You may reinforce skills taught in therapy sessions by practicing articulation exercises, fine motor activities, or sensory integration techniques during daily classroom routines.

Additionally, ensuring students attend their therapy sessions on time and are prepared to participate helps maximize the benefits of these services.

- **Providing personal care:** Some students require assistance with daily living activities, such as mobility, feeding, hygiene, or toilet use. You may need to help a student move between classrooms, use assistive devices, or complete self-care tasks while promoting as much independence as possible. These responsibilities require patience, sensitivity, and a deep understanding of each student's individual needs. Encouraging students to build these essential life skills helps foster their long-term independence and confidence.

Being aware of each student's IEP goals, accommodations, and services is the key to providing effective support. The IEP serves as a road map for a student's educational growth, and as a paraprofessional, you are an essential part of implementing that plan. By following the guidance outlined in the IEP, offering encouragement, and adapting your support to meet each student's unique needs, you help pave the way for their success. With your dedication, patience, and commitment, you'll witness incredible progress and be a crucial part of each student's journey toward achieving their goals.

> Being aware of each student's IEP goals, accommodations, and services is the key to providing effective support. The IEP serves as a road map for a student's educational growth, and as a paraprofessional, you are an essential part of implementing that plan.

## Understanding the Continuum of Special Education Placements

In special education, there are different levels of special education services, referred to as the continuum of special education services. This continuum ranges from least restrictive to most restrictive environments, with the ultimate goal being to provide each student with the appropriate level of support to succeed academically and socially. (See figure 3.2.) Another goal is to have the student get the least restrictive environment possible. At the least restrictive end of the continuum are general education classrooms, where students with special needs are included in the same classroom as their typically developing peers. This setting allows for maximum inclusion and opportunities for socialization.

As the level of support needed increases, students may be placed in resource rooms or self-contained classrooms, where they receive more individual attention and support from special education teachers and paraprofessionals. When students

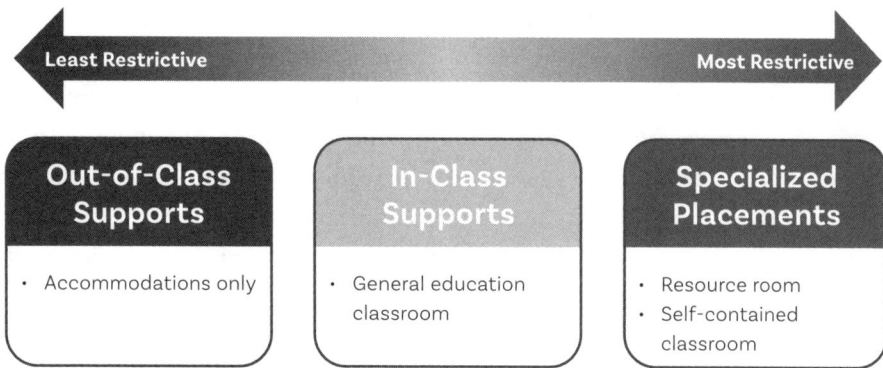

**Figure 3.2: Continuum of student needs.**

are in these more structured or specialized environments, the goal is still to include them in general education settings whenever possible. This may involve their participation in certain classes, school activities, or social events alongside their peers without disabilities. These inclusive opportunities can promote academic growth, peer connections, and a stronger sense of belonging.

As a special education paraprofessional, you may be asked to help mainstream students into general education classes. To effectively support these students, you must be clear on what the purpose of mainstreaming is, what the goals of the mainstreaming experience are per the students' IEP goals, and what each day's schedule will look like. Mainstreaming might produce anxiety in a student because it is new and the student does not know what to expect. By being gentle but firm with students and reassuring them, you can help them through their mainstreaming time. Once you are in the general education classroom, you and your student might find that the classroom is louder or busier than what you're accustomed to. Do your best to help your student participate where they can. When it is too much, gently remove them or sit next to them to reassure the student that you are there and everyone is learning together.

## Understanding the Continuum of Paraprofessional Placements

Understanding the continuum of paraprofessional placements is also important. Since the continuum for students ranges from least restrictive to most restrictive environments, with each placement offering different levels of support and services, the various levels of work for paraprofessionals mirror that continuum. Usually, paraprofessionals working in the most restrictive environments receive higher compensation, because some of their job duties and job knowledge requirements are more strenuous than those of other paraprofessional jobs in less restrictive environments. For example, the paraprofessionals working with special education students who need the highest level of support may be required to help students with the toilet, change diapers, and help feed students lunch or snacks. Many districts will give paraprofessional roles different titles that clarify the level of paraprofessional and the expected amount of support.

## Understanding Confidentiality

Confidentiality is an important aspect of working with students who have special needs. Maintaining confidentiality means respecting the privacy of the student and their family and any sensitive information that may be shared with you as a paraprofessional. This includes information about the student's disability, IEP, behavior plan, and health plan, as well as any other personal information. You must keep this information confidential and share it only with those who need to know. Keeping their personal information confidential creates a safe and trusting environment for the students to learn and grow. As a paraprofessional, you have a responsibility to protect the privacy and dignity of the students you work with, and maintaining confidentiality is a vital part of fulfilling that responsibility.

To maintain confidentiality, use care when handling and sharing information about the students you work with. Avoid discussing sensitive information in public or with colleagues who do not have a legitimate reason to know. Keep any physical or electronic records secure, and only access them when necessary for your job duties. If you have any questions about confidentiality issues, speak to a supervisor so you can continue learning and ensure you do the right thing.

Maintaining confidentiality can be challenging when others approach you and ask you questions. Table 3.1 shows some of the tricky questions or comments that can come your way and how you can best respond to keep confidentiality.

## Addressing the Needs of Students With Medical Conditions or Chronic Health Issues

Addressing the needs of students with medical conditions or chronic health issues in the classroom requires a thoughtful and proactive approach. These students most likely have unique challenges that impact their ability to fully participate in classroom activities, so paraprofessionals must understand their needs and provide them

**Table 3.1: Responses That Maintain Confidentiality**

| Comment From Another Person | Your Possible Confidential Response |
|---|---|
| "Hey, I heard you are working at ABC School. Some people have said that there are a lot of suspensions there. Is that true?" | "I'm not able to discuss staff or student matters, but I can say the school works hard to support all students in a safe learning environment." |
| "I heard the office manager was really upset after talking to a student's parent. What happened?" | "I'm sorry, I can't discuss any situation that involves students or families." |
| "I heard the office manager is getting a divorce. Have you heard anything?" | "As an employee, I am not allowed to talk about other employees outside of school. Sorry." |
| "My daughter is in Ms. Smith's class, and there is a student in there who you work with who is really distracting. Can we get that student out of the classroom?" | "Student progress is confidential. I can't discuss these kinds of things." |

with timely support. Research shows that approximately 25 percent of children ages two to eight have chronic health issues, such as allergies, asthma, and obesity, and that having chronic health issues can result in poorer academic achievement (National Center for Chronic Disease Prevention and Health Promotion, 2017).

If a student's health problems impact their academic learning, their IEP can include a health plan. This plan outlines any accommodations or medical interventions required during the school day. For example, a student with type 1 diabetes might have a health plan that allows for scheduled blood sugar checks, access to snacks, and permission to visit the nurse as needed. As you get to know the student and their health needs, you can ensure that the student's health needs are being met and that the student can fully engage in the learning process.

Health issues that can warrant a health plan include the following. When working with students with medical conditions or chronic health issues, paraprofessionals should be prepared for potential challenges. You need to be knowledgeable about your student's condition and any possible symptoms or complications during the school day.

- **Chronic illnesses:** These conditions, like asthma, diabetes, epilepsy, seizures, and heart conditions, require ongoing medical management and medication, which makes a health plan an important component of the student's IEP. The health plan ensures that staff are aware of warning signs, know how to respond during a medical episode, and can support the student to safely participate in classroom and school activities.

- **Allergies:** Students with severe allergies to foods, medications, or insect stings might need an EpiPen or other emergency medications, and a health plan can help for any emergency situations at the school site. The plan should include clear instructions on how to avoid exposure, when to administer medication, and who is trained to respond. This will help prevent medical emergencies and ensure rapid intervention if needed.

- **Mental health conditions:** Anxiety, depression, and ADHD are becoming increasingly common in students and may warrant a health plan if a student's learning is being negatively impacted by their mental health condition. If the mental health condition is the primary reason that the student qualifies for special education, it will be addressed through the IEP itself under an eligibility category such as emotional disturbance or other health impairment. However, if the condition is not the primary eligibility reason but still affects the student's day-to-day functioning (for example, they need breaks, counseling, or medication), those supports can be documented in a health plan and attached to the IEP to ensure coordinated care throughout the school day.

- **Accidents and injuries:** Any student can experience unexpected accidents or injuries that require medical attention. If a student's recovery will take a while and it might impact their learning, a health plan can be used to outline what support and help that student will receive to ensure they don't fall behind. For example, a student recovering from a broken leg may need mobility accommodations, longer passing periods, or access to remote learning if they will be absent for an extended period.

- **Vision and hearing challenges:** Students who need corrective lenses or hearing aids benefit from a health plan. The plan can outline ongoing additional support that these students need to be successful in the classroom. This may include preferential seating, assistive technology, visual aids, or collaboration with specialists such as audiologists or teachers of the visually impaired.

## Helping Students With Physical Disabilities Access the Curriculum and School Environment

Assisting students with physical disabilities to access the curriculum and school environment is crucial for ensuring these students have equal opportunities for success in the educational setting. Be proactive in understanding the challenges that these students face so you can identify and implement strategies to support their learning and overall school experience. Ensuring that students with physical disabilities have access to the curriculum in a way that meets their specific needs is a key aspect of your work. This is where you come in, ensuring they have everything they need in order to learn.

For example, a student who struggles with verbal language might use a speech-generating device or communication app to answer questions, participate in discussions, or express preferences. A student with limited hand mobility might use adaptive keyboards or touch screens instead of traditional writing tools. Others may benefit from audiobooks, enlarged print, or speech-to-text software to support their reading and writing access. Also, you may have a student who is hearing impaired and has an assistive technology device to help them communicate their needs. By getting to know this student and understanding how their device works, you will be able to open up communication for them to better meet their needs.

As a dedicated paraprofessional, you can support accessibility by assisting with day-to-day logistics and advocating for student needs. While you may not have the authority to make structural changes, you play an essential role in noticing barriers, communicating concerns to the team, and collaborating on practical solutions. This may involve working with the classroom teacher to modify the classroom layout, providing additional support for navigating the school halls, or ensuring that assistive devices are readily available. Collaboration with other school staff, such as physical therapists, occupational therapists, and special education teachers, can also help when supporting students with physical disabilities.

## Supporting Students With Autism Spectrum Disorder

Working with students who have autism spectrum disorder may mean that you face unique challenges in providing support and creating an inclusive learning environment. Understanding the individual needs of each student with autism allows you to develop solid strategies to help them experience success. The Centers for Disease Control and Prevention (CDC, 2024) outlines common characteristics of autistic students, such as difficulty with social communication and interaction, including challenges with making eye contact, understanding social cues, or forming peer relationships. Some students may show strong preferences for routines, engage in repetitive behaviors, or become intensely focused on particular interests. These traits can be accompanied by unique strengths and deep connections with trusted individuals.

You can support autistic students by implementing structured strategies that promote consistency and understanding in the classroom. Talk with your classroom teacher about using the following best practices (Gavin, 2018; Maki et al., 2022).

- **Use visual supports:** Provide visual schedules, picture cues, and step-by-step instructions to help students anticipate their daily activities and transitions. These tools reduce anxiety, increase independence, and make expectations clearer. Visuals might include individual desk schedules, labeled bins, or first–then boards that outline task sequences.

- **Establish structured routines:** Maintain a consistent daily schedule to create a sense of security and predictability for students. When the schedule remains stable, students are better able to regulate themselves and focus on learning. Even small classroom routines, like greeting time or cleanup procedures, should be practiced and reinforced consistently.

- **Implement positive reinforcement:** Work with the classroom teacher to decide on and use praise, rewards, or token systems to encourage positive behaviors and reinforce expected actions. Appropriate rewards can include small tangible items (like stickers or pencils), preferred activities (like extra computer time or completion of a chosen classroom job), or social rewards (like verbal praise or a note home). Token systems, such as earning stars, points, or chips toward a chosen reward, help students understand the link between their actions and positive outcomes.

- **Reduce surprises:** Prepare students for any changes in routine by providing advance notice and visual or verbal cues. For example, if there is a school assembly or substitute teacher, show a picture or social story ahead of time and explain what to expect. This helps students manage transitions with less anxiety.

- **Encourage socialization:** Facilitate peer interactions through structured activities and guided group work to help students build social skills. Role plays, turn-taking games, and small-group discussions give students chances to build communication and cooperation skills in a supportive environment. Paraprofessionals can model language, prompt social engagement, and celebrate small steps toward connection.

- **Mainstream students when possible:** Inclusion in general education settings can provide opportunities for social development, engagement with peers, and peer modeling. For autistic students, mainstreaming is typically outlined in their IEPs, which specify the appropriate placement and level of support. Paraprofessionals should follow the IEP guidance and work in coordination with the classroom teacher and special education team to ensure a student's needs are met in an inclusive setting.

- **Be patient and flexible:** Understand that each student has unique needs and may require individualized approaches to succeed. Progress may look different for every learner, as what works well for one student may not work for another. Give grace, stay curious, and celebrate each step forward.

Autistic students bring valuable strengths, interests, and perspectives to the classroom. By meeting them where they are, proactively supporting their needs, and honoring their unique gifts, you help create a classroom culture that values inclusion, respect, and growth for all students.

## Addressing Communication Barriers for Students With Speech and Language Impairments

Communication barriers can pose significant challenges for students who have speech and language impairments. These students may struggle to effectively communicate their thoughts and ideas, leading to frustration and feelings of isolation. The American Speech-Language-Hearing Association (n.d.) points out the importance of early detection of language and speech issues so that there can be early intervention and assistance. Language and speech issues can range from having a hard time pronouncing certain sounds to stuttering or being unable to communicate one's thoughts or emotions clearly. The American Speech-Language-Hearing Association (n.d.) encourages a robust speech program where a speech-language pathologist and trained paraprofessionals can work with students on these specific skills.

An effective strategy for addressing severe communication barriers is to provide alternative communication methods. These may include augmentative and alternative communication (AAC) devices, picture communication boards, or sign language. AAC devices, such as speech-generating devices or apps, enable nonverbal students to effectively express their needs and thoughts. Picture communication boards offer a visual way for students to select and convey messages, which reduces frustration and enhances comprehension. Sign language can also be a powerful tool for students to develop a consistent and accessible means of communication.

Paraprofessionals are not expected to independently master these tools, but they do play a vital role in helping students use their tools throughout the school day. Working closely with a student's speech-language pathologist, special education teacher, and family, paraprofessionals can ensure the communication strategies used are consistent, appropriate, and aligned with the student's individual needs. In some cases, a paraprofessional may receive basic training in how to support sign language or AAC use as directed by the IEP team.

Working closely with speech-language pathologists is important for determining the most appropriate communication method for each student. The more a student is reminded of their learning strategies, the better their long-term outcomes will be. Also, to make the classroom more inclusive, you can implement strategies that improve the overall communication environment. These may involve reducing background noise, speaking slowly, using visual aids, and providing repeated opportunities for students to practice their communication skills. A safe, trusting environment will help students practice communication skills more comfortably. After all, do we talk more when we are in a safe and comfortable environment? Yes, we do.

As you gain more experience working with students with special needs, you will gain techniques, strategies, and knowledge to help you work with a wide range of students. It takes a lot of dedication, effort, and passion to work with students who come to school with significant challenges. You are their advocate and their communicator. You are their bridge to living an everyday life as much as possible. You are their superhero!

## Meet Sarah: Building Bridges Through Understanding

Arjun, a second grader diagnosed with autism spectrum disorder, is bright and curious. He struggles with social cues, nonverbal communication, and sensory information processing. Loud noises and crowded spaces can overwhelm him, leading to meltdowns or withdrawal. Traditional classroom settings often challenge Arjun's ability to focus and participate.

Sarah, a paraprofessional who has experience working with children with autism spectrum disorder, recognizes the importance of building trust and establishing a safe space for Arjun. Here's how she shows her superhero skills.

- **Communication:** Sarah learns alternative communication methods, such as picture cards and simple phrases, to understand Arjun's needs and preferences.

- **Routine and structure:** Sarah develops a visual schedule with clear expectations, which helps Arjun anticipate transitions and reduces his anxiety.

- **Positive reinforcement:** Sarah praises Arjun's efforts and celebrates even small achievements to boost his confidence and motivation.

- **Sensory awareness:** Sarah adjusts the classroom environment to decrease sensory overload. She provides tools like noise-canceling headphones and fidget toys to help Arjun self-regulate as needed.

- **Social interaction:** Sarah understands the importance of social interaction for Arjun's development. She has him interact with peers in small, structured groups and offers guidance and support during interactions.

With Sarah's consistent support, Arjun begins to thrive. He becomes more verbal, effectively uses his picture cards, and participates more actively in class. Most importantly, he begins to initiate interactions with peers, demonstrating growing confidence, stronger social skills, and reduced anxiety. Sarah's dedication to and understanding of Arjun's needs significantly improve his social interaction, communication skills, and classroom engagement.

As Arjun moves into the upper-elementary grades, the strategies Sarah put in place continue to support his growth. Her collaboration with teachers, specialists, and Arjun's family created a strong foundation that helps him successfully transition from grade to grade. Sarah's role didn't just make a difference in second grade; it helped set Arjun up for lasting success in school and beyond.

## Wrap-Up

This chapter covered the different types of disabilities, the importance of the IEP document, and how paraprofessionals can best support and work with students with autism and other specific disabilities. In the feature box that follows, you'll find practical advice from experienced special education paraprofessionals. Their insights are grounded in day-to-day experience. Then, in the "Notes and Reflections: Supporting Students With Special Needs" reproducible (page 59), you'll have the opportunity to thoughtfully reflect on what you've learned and consider how these insights apply to your own practice.

## *Advice From*
### SUPERHERO PARAPROFESSIONALS

"Patience is key. Every student learns differently, and those with special needs may need more time or a different approach to grasp a concept. Celebrate small victories and focus on building a positive relationship based on trust, structure, and understanding."

— V. Sweeny, personal communication, November 5, 2024

"Collaboration is crucial. Don't be afraid to ask for help from teachers, therapists, or other specialists. Working together as a team can create a better support system that addresses each student's needs."

— E. Gomez, personal communication, May 30, 2024

"Focus on their strengths. Every student has something they're good at, even if it's not what's traditionally seen as 'academic.' Help them build confidence by recognizing their unique talents and encouraging them to explore their interests."

— K. Romney, personal communication, August 30, 2024

# Notes and Reflections: Supporting Students With Special Needs

Take a few moments to reflect on the following questions about being a superhero paraprofessional.

1. What key responsibilities would you have as a paraprofessional working with students with IEPs?

2. How can you clearly communicate with teachers and other staff to best support these students?

3. Reflect on the different levels of support in your school and how paraprofessionals are involved in each. Where do you see yourself fitting into this continuum? What additional training or skills might you need to be effective in that role?

4. How can you advocate for students with special needs in the classroom and school environment?

5. What would be the most rewarding part of working with students with special needs?

# Supporting Students With Behavioral and Attention Challenges

If you are in a school long enough, you will probably hear someone say that student behaviors are out of control. "Kids didn't act this way when I was in school," they say. But if given enough time to reflect, most of us can remember the "troublemakers" in our childhood classrooms—those students who caused problems for other students or made fun of the teacher just to make the class laugh. Some students didn't follow directions or had too much energy to sit all day. Students are kids, and they come from many different homes and parenting styles. We cannot control what students are exposed to in their homes, how they are taught to behave or not to behave, or whether they come to school ready to learn and follow the rules. What we can control is learning as much as we can about behaviors and how to teach, train, and reward students for good behavior.

## KEY POINTS

- Recognize common behavioral issues in students.
- Focus on the ABCs of behavior.
- Understand how to work in a school with or without a schoolwide management system.
- Use positive and proactive superhero strategies.
- Work with students with attention challenges.

Good behavior is directly associated with better academic learning and social skills, so becoming a behavior specialist is in your best interest. A study by researchers from the University of Missouri concludes that disruption declines and academic achievement increases when students receive positive encouragement and very clear behavioral expectations instead of feedback that focuses only on negative behaviors (Consiglio, 2021). Those results are encouraging and also point us in the direction of mastering working with students who struggle with their behaviors.

This chapter presents the impacts and causes of behavioral challenges, common behavioral issues in students, the ABC approach to behaviors and considerations for behavior management, positive and proactive strategies for behavior management, nonverbal and visual cues for positive behavioral support, and support for students with escalated needs.

## The Learning Impact and Causes of Behavioral Challenges

The frequency and severity of behavioral challenges appear to be on the rise in classrooms. In 2023, more than 70 percent of teachers reported an increase in disruptive behavior in the classroom, compared to 66 percent in 2019 (Prothero, 2023). Even if such behaviors weren't on the rise, the impact of any behavioral challenge on learning is still a significant concern for educators. Students who exhibit behavioral issues often struggle to engage in the learning process, leading to academic setbacks and emotional distress. If a student is not paying attention, not completing assignments, and disrupting class routines, they will quickly fall behind academically.

Students with higher rates of challenging behavior often experience lower academic achievement (Blank & Shavit, 2016). In a study of 1,400 elementary general education and special education teachers, the IRIS Center (2020) reports that disruptive behaviors account for 2.4 hours of lost instruction each week. Over the course of a year, this translates to almost three weeks of lost instructional time. The IRIS Center finds that behavioral issues result in the following, in addition to lost instructional time.

- Lowered academic achievement for the disruptive students and their classmates
- Lowered sense of belonging at school
- Decreased student engagement and motivation
- Teacher stress and frustration
- Teacher turnover

This is why the role of paraprofessionals is critical; by helping these students with their behavioral challenges, they help them stay caught up academically, reducing their overall frustration levels. However, providing this help requires understanding the underlying cause of the challenging behavior.

It is usually apparent when a student is experiencing behavioral challenges. They typically stand out from other students in their behaviors and attitudes or how they respond to others. It is important to understand that misbehavior is a form of communication, and these students express themselves through their behaviors. They are letting others know they have unmet needs or wants; they are unable to raise their hand nicely, wait to be called on, and verbally tell us what is wrong and how they need help. Students with behavioral challenges are not yet in a place in their growth where they can do those things, and their behaviors are their main line of communication.

With this perspective, it may be easier to realize that misbehavior is not personal. A student acting out in some way is not intentionally trying to cause trouble or inconvenience. As trauma-informed education research has shown (Substance Abuse and Mental Health Services Administration [SAMHSA], 2014), many student behaviors are rooted in deeper emotional, neurological, or environmental needs. Oftentimes, the root cause of their behavior is related to trauma, sensory issues, unmet needs, home issues, or learning differences. By keeping this in mind, you can approach students with behavioral challenges with more empathy, compassion, and care as you help them express their needs in different, more positive ways.

## Common Behavioral Issues in Students

In the educational setting, students may exhibit a variety of behavioral challenges that disrupt learning, create tension in the classroom, and impact the well-being of both students and staff. Findings by the Pew Research Center (Lin, Parker, & Horowitz, 2024) highlight growing concerns among educators about the frequency and impact of behavioral challenges in schools. While every student is unique, certain patterns of behavior are commonly observed in classrooms. Drawing from widely observed trends in classroom behavior and best practices in education, the following challenges are among the most common (Lin et al., 2024).

- **Disruptive and attention-seeking behaviors:** Some students struggle with impulse control and self-regulation, leading them to engage in behaviors that disrupt the flow of instruction. Excessively talking, interrupting the teacher, making noises, or engaging in off-task activities (such as using a phone, doodling, or tapping on a desk) can prevent both the individual and their peers from fully participating in learning. Attention-seeking behaviors often involve attempts to draw reactions from others. Some students crack jokes at inappropriate times, make exaggerated gestures, or call out answers without being called on. These students may feed off the responses they receive, whether positive or negative. Disrespectful behaviors, such as arguing with the teacher, challenging authority, or disregarding classroom rules, can escalate if not addressed appropriately.

- **Aggression:** Aggressive behaviors can manifest in different forms, including physical aggression (hitting, kicking, pushing, and so on) and verbal aggression (yelling, calling people names, or making threats). Some students engage in passive-aggressive behaviors, such as intentionally annoying peers, refusing to participate, or using sarcasm to provoke others. Students who are frustrated, have difficulty regulating their emotions, or feel misunderstood may behave aggressively. Some students lash out when they feel cornered, while others may exhibit reactive aggression in response to perceived slights or challenges from their peers. If unchecked, these behaviors can escalate into bullying, intimidation, or ongoing conflict, leading to a hostile classroom environment.

- **Noncompliance and defiance:** Noncompliant students ignore requests, refuse to follow instructions, or exhibit passive resistance by doing the opposite of what is expected. Defiant behavior may escalate into verbal arguments, blatant refusal to participate, or intentional disruption of lessons. Defiance can stem from various sources, such as a desire for control, frustration with authority, or difficulty managing emotions. Some students use defiance as a coping mechanism, testing boundaries to gauge how much control they have over their environment. These behaviors can create significant power struggles between students and educators, often leading to escalating conflicts if they're not managed effectively.

- **Attention issues:** Students who struggle with sustained attention may frequently lose focus, become distracted by their surroundings, or shift between tasks without completing them. These students may miss instructions, fail to retain key information, or have difficulty following multistep directions. Transitions between activities or locations can be particularly challenging, as it may take students with attention difficulties longer to shift their focus. This challenge is often compounded for students with sensory processing difficulties or executive function deficits, which make it difficult for them to stay engaged without additional structure.

- **Hyperactivity:** Hyperactive students exhibit excessive movement that makes it difficult for them to remain seated or focused for extended periods. They may fidget, tap on their desks, rock in their chairs, or frequently get up and move around. These behaviors can interfere with their own learning as well as their classmates' ability to concentrate. Some students display hyperactivity in bursts, while others appear to be in a constant state of restlessness, struggling to stay still for even short periods. If students do not have structured ways to channel their energy, they may become increasingly disruptive.

- **Withdrawal:** While some students act out, others withdraw socially or emotionally, choosing to disengage from classroom activities, group work, or discussions. These students may avoid eye contact, sit alone, or refrain from speaking in class. Withdrawal can be a sign of social anxiety, low self-esteem, past negative experiences, or emotional distress. Some students fear making mistakes or being judged by their peers, while others may feel disconnected from their classmates. In some cases, withdrawal can be linked to depression, trauma, or a history of exclusion, making it difficult for students to engage meaningfully.

- **Difficulty managing emotions:** Students with emotional regulation difficulties may experience intense mood swings, meltdowns, or emotional outbursts that disrupt the classroom. Some may cry, scream, or shut down when overwhelmed, while others struggle to express their frustration appropriately. For some students, triggers are unpredictable, leading to sudden emotional reactions that catch educators and peers off guard. Other students may exhibit consistent patterns of dysregulation and struggle to recover from setbacks or process emotions in a healthy way. Over time, these challenges can have a negative impact on academic performance, peer relationships, and overall well-being.

- **Communication challenges:** Students with communication difficulties may struggle to express their thoughts, needs, or concerns effectively. Some may have difficulty forming complete sentences, finding the right words, or responding appropriately in conversations. For students with language disorders, autism, or other developmental differences, these challenges can lead to frustration, social misunderstandings, or behavioral outbursts when they feel unheard or misinterpreted. Some students rely on nonverbal communication, such as gestures, physical actions, or assistive technology.

- **Task avoidance:** Task avoidance is a common challenge where students procrastinate, refuse to start assignments, or create distractions to escape work. These students may wander around the room, make excuses, or repeatedly ask to leave for the restroom or water fountain. These behaviors can stem from low confidence, anxiety, fear of failure, or executive function difficulties. Some students become overwhelmed by assignments they perceive as too difficult, while others lack the intrinsic motivation to engage in academic tasks.

- **Peer conflict:** Interpersonal challenges among students can lead to frequent disagreements, arguments, and even bullying behaviors. Some students struggle with boundaries, social cues, or sharing, which leads to tension in group settings. Others misinterpret social interactions, reacting defensively to perceived slights or exclusion. Conflicts can manifest in verbal disputes, physical altercations, or ongoing relational aggression, such as gossip, exclusion, or intimidation. Unresolved social conflicts can significantly impact classroom dynamics, leading to tension and distraction for all students involved.

By learning about these behavioral challenges, you can better understand the root causes of students' actions and how they impact the classroom environment. While every student's situation is unique, understanding these common behaviors allows educators to anticipate challenges and create structured, supportive, and responsive learning environments that address the diverse needs of all students.

## The ABC Lens for Behaviors and Considerations for Behavior Management

One helpful way of looking at and analyzing behaviors is using the ABCs of behavior. In *The Paraprofessional's Guide to Effective Behavioral Intervention*, Betty Y. Ashbaker and Jill Morgan (2015) share the ABC approach to working with students with behavioral issues. This strategy focuses on analyzing behaviors through the ABC lens.

- **A is the antecedent:** The antecedent is what happened before the behavior occurred. What triggered the behavior? For example, another student came up to the student, took their pencil, and walked away. That triggered the student to get up and angrily push the other student. Finding the antecedent involves taking the time to observe and analyze the patterns of behavior exhibited by the student, as well as to consider environmental factors that may have contributed to their reaction. It also involves asking questions and listening to those who were involved in or witnessed the event. Things to analyze include the environment, demands put on the student, stimuli, and outside factors like health, sleep, or hunger.

- **B is the behavior:** A student's behavior is what they do in reaction to the antecedent. In this example, the student pushed the other student to the ground after they took the pencil. Things to document about the behavior include its duration, intensity, and frequency. Many times, the behavior is a direct reaction to the antecedent.

- **C is the consequence:** The consequence is what happens after the behavior. The classroom teacher or school administrator decides on implications, although they may talk with you, the paraprofessional involved with the student, about what consequence makes the most sense. The goal of consequences is to teach the student the correct behavior and help them not repeat the incorrect behavior in the future.

Following the ABC process can take the emotions out of a behavioral incident and let you instead focus on the facts and how best to move forward with a student. Starting with the antecedent and figuring out what caused the emotions or behavior is a powerful and effective way of analyzing behavioral issues. It positions you to be proactive, as you can determine what the trigger was for that student and then work to help them react better the next time that trigger happens. Now that is powerful learning!

As a paraprofessional, you need to understand that behavior systems may vary—some are schoolwide, while others are specific to individual classrooms. Learning the systems already in place in both environments is key to supporting consistency and student success. When they are working in the classroom, paraprofessionals must be conscious of their approach to discipline, especially if they are working with very young (preK–K) students. The following sections discuss each of these factors in more detail.

### Schoolwide Management System

A schoolwide system is a shared set of rules and behavioral expectations that are consistently applied across the entire school. A growing body of research demonstrates that schoolwide behavior management frameworks, such as Positive Behavioral Interventions and Supports (PBIS), are highly effective in fostering positive student outcomes; their consistency helps improve student behavior (Hawken, Vincent, & Schumann, 2020; Reina et al., 2023). When implemented with fidelity, these systems can reduce disruptive behaviors, office discipline referrals, and suspensions, while also improving academic performance and students' social-emotional well-being (Childs, Kincaid, George, & Gage, 2015; Hierck & Weber, 2025; Reina et al., 2023).

PBIS is a proactive approach to behavior management that focuses on teaching students appropriate behaviors rather than simply reacting to inappropriate ones. One key aspect of PBIS is establishing clear expectations for behavior. Educators work with students to develop a set of expectations that are positively stated and easy to understand; these can be consistently reinforced through positive reinforcement and praise. By clearly defining expectations and providing positive reinforcement, you can help students understand what is expected of them and encourage them to exhibit positive behaviors.

Another critical aspect of PBIS is creating a system of rewards and consequences. Schools can establish rewards, such as praise, stickers, or extra privileges, for students who demonstrate positive behaviors. At the same time, consequences need to be fair, consistent, and proportional to any negative behaviors. With this combination of rewards and consequences, students gain motivation to exhibit positive behaviors and discourage negative ones.

When you join a classroom, ask about the system already in place to support behavioral instruction and reinforcement, and work within that system. Visit the Center on PBIS's website (www.pbis.org) to access PBIS tools and resources.

### Classroom-Only Management System

If you work in a school that does not have a schoolwide management system, the classroom management system becomes even more critical. In a well-managed classroom, several components are in place for students to be successful.

- Clear routines and schedules are taught so students are aware of them.
- Classroom rules are set, and all students know what is expected of them.

- Appropriate behavior is taught to students and not just expected of them.

- In this safe environment, students know they are not expected to be perfect, but they are expected to learn to meet behavioral expectations.

It is the teacher's responsibility to have these components in place and teach students about them. The classrooms with these critical components are much easier to work in as a paraprofessional because expectations are explicit. But there may be times when you are in a classroom with unclear expectations. This is a much more challenging situation for you to operate within. Since it is not your classroom, there isn't much you can do other than ask the teacher what the rules and expectations are because they are unclear to you.

If you find yourself working with small groups or individual students, you can set up your own behavioral expectations and routines and teach students that when they work with you, these expectations are in place. The general rule is to have a maximum of three to six expectations and positively express them. For example, instead of saying, "Don't touch other students," you can say, "Keep your hands to yourself." Make sure to discuss these rules with the students and let them process them and ask any questions or make comments. Let's say your name is Mrs. Brooks. Your paraprofessional rules could be called "Mrs. Brooks's List of Rules" or "Mrs. Brooks's Small-Group Rules." Figure 4.1 shows sample rules for working with students in small groups.

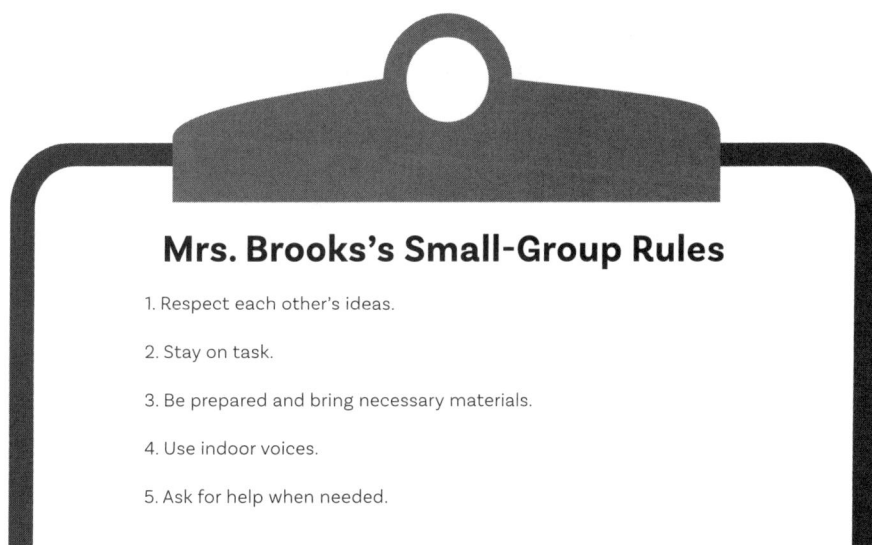

**Mrs. Brooks's Small-Group Rules**

1. Respect each other's ideas.

2. Stay on task.

3. Be prepared and bring necessary materials.

4. Use indoor voices.

5. Ask for help when needed.

**Figure 4.1: Sample rules for working with students in small groups.**

### Conscious Discipline

An approach that continues to grow in popularity and effectiveness is Conscious Discipline®, created by Becky A. Bailey (2021). This adult-first approach to self-regulation integrates social-emotional learning, theory and application, equitable school culture, and research- and brain-based discipline practices. The Conscious Discipline approach is founded on the knowledge that students and adults have the following three states of being (Bailey, 2021).

1. **Survival:** When students are in the survival state, they are in fight, flight, or freeze mode, and they usually behave in physically aggressive ways, throw tantrums, or shut down. What they need most is safety.

2. **Emotional:** In the emotional state, students seek attention, are resistant, resort to name calling and other verbal behavior, and greatly need connection with a safe adult.

3. **Executive:** In the executive state, students are willing to problem-solve and reach a resolution to their conflict, and they are in need of help to solve their problem. The hope is that both the students and you, as the paraprofessional, aim to work daily in the executive state.

One of the most powerful components of this approach is the importance of being aware of our own emotional states and needs as the adults in the room working with students. If we are not self-regulated, how can we ask students to be? Therefore, we work on being adults who show composure and empathy as well as love and acceptance of the students we work with.

> One of the most powerful components of the Conscious Discipline approach is the importance of being aware of our own emotional states and needs as the adults in the room working with students.

The Conscious Discipline approach requires deeply understanding where students are coming from and helping them move from the survival state to the emotional state and, hopefully, to the executive state, where they can best learn. Paraprofessionals do this by providing students with feelings of safety, connection, and, eventually, self-empowerment to problem-solve for themselves.

### Work With Very Young Students

As preschool and transitional kindergarten programs are growing, the number of paraprofessionals who support our youngest learners is increasing. At these young ages, emotional regulation can be challenging for students as they learn to navigate the classroom environment. Preschoolers often have limited vocabulary to express their feelings, and their impulse control is still developing, making it difficult for them to manage strong emotions like frustration, anger, or sadness. These early years are crucial in developing the social-emotional skills that students will carry with them throughout their academic careers.

If you work with these young learners, you must create a structured, supportive, and nurturing environment for them. You need to implement strategies that help them feel safe and understood, offering guidance through routines, positive reinforcement, and redirection when needed. Creating a predictable schedule, using visual supports, and modeling appropriate emotional responses can aid you in calming a student when they feel overwhelmed. Additionally, understanding the importance of individualized attention and patience is key. Students each have unique needs, and their ability to regulate their emotions varies. Building strong, trusting relationships with the students supports their social-emotional growth while encouraging peer interactions and teaching them problem-solving skills that can also promote positive social behaviors in the classroom.

Working with really young students is very rewarding while also being very challenging. By helping these students develop emotional regulation and coping mechanisms early on, you can create a peaceful classroom environment and also lay the foundation for the children's future in school and beyond. You are with them at the start of a long journey in their education and can set them up for long-term success both academically and socially. Now that is superhero work!

## Positive and Proactive Strategies for Behavior Management

It is tempting to react to challenging behaviors with punishments and reprimands since many of us were raised with that approach. However, research shows that punishments and reprimands do very little to help students find more positive behaviors. In his article "To Fix Students' Bad Behavior, Stop Punishing Them," Wayne D'Orio (2023) argues that punitive discipline models are ineffective and often counterproductive in addressing student misbehavior. He references research indicating that traditional punishment not only fails to change behavior long-term but may exacerbate feelings of disconnection and alienation from school. Studies show that exclusionary practices like suspensions, expulsions, and zero-tolerance policies do not improve safety or academic outcomes and instead contribute to long-term negative psychosocial effects (APA Zero-Tolerance Task Force Review; NASP Center, 2023). Punitive responses can fuel what psychologists term a *vicious stress cycle*, in which punitive discipline increases stress, hinders skill development, and escalates future behavior (Ablon, 2020).

Rather than punishing students for misbehavior, D'Orio and the research he shares recommend trauma-informed, empathetic alternatives that emphasize teaching self-regulation, restoring relationships, and building student agency through collaborative and restorative approaches. In turn, these alternatives can help you build trust and rapport with students toward more successful interactions and outcomes (D'Orio, 2023).

The causes of misbehavior come from weaknesses in one of four areas: (1) flexibility and adaptability, (2) frustration tolerance, (3) problem-solving skills, and (4) emotional regulation (D'Orio, 2023). Looking at student behaviors through the framing of these four areas allows you to approach a behavioral situation with a win-win mentality and seek to understand the student's perspective before demanding compliance.

Let's take a closer look at the four areas that you must strengthen in students to improve their behavioral skills and strategies.

1. **Flexibility and adaptability:** This refers to the ability to adjust to changes in routines, unexpected challenges, or new ways of thinking. Students who struggle with behavior often have difficulty adapting to change and may require additional support to build resilience.

2. **Frustration tolerance:** This refers to the capacity to persist through challenges without becoming overwhelmed. Many students who struggle with frustration may have outbursts, react with avoidance, or give up easily.

3. **Problem-solving skills:** This refers to the ability to identify issues, generate possible solutions, evaluate outcomes, and make thoughtful decisions. Strong problem-solving skills help students navigate social situations and academic challenges more effectively.

4. **Emotional regulation:** This refers to the skill of recognizing, understanding, and appropriately managing emotions. Students who have difficulty with emotional regulation may have intense reactions to setbacks and struggle to calm down independently.

What follows are some specific strategies that can help you with these four important areas for improving student behavior.

### Consistency

When behavioral issues stem from students' inability to be flexible and adaptable, consistency is a lifeline for them. Many students who struggle behaviorally crave and thrive with consistency and clear expectations. This consistency helps students feel safe and cared for. They learn that they can rely on the adults at school, and they know they have a daily routine to follow. Without a daily routine and consistency from the adults, students may feel anxious and act out because they are unsettled.

Being a consistent and caring adult for students is a meaningful part of serving as a paraprofessional. One way you can be consistent with students is by using positive reinforcement. When you consistently reinforce the positive choices they make or the effort they are giving, students will realize that you are on their side and want them to do well. No one system or model works for all students, but by consistently showing up for your students and getting to know what makes them tick, you can design a reinforcement system that works for them.

### Relationship-Based Responses

Working with students with behavioral challenges begins with building a rapport and connection. These students are used to adults telling them they are wrong or acting badly. If you start on a positive note with a student and they feel like you care and want to help them, you are well on your way to addressing their behavioral issues positively and productively.

Get to know the student and ask them questions about their interests and hobbies. Let them get to know you a bit as well. Here are some questions you can ask; adjust them depending on your student's age.

- "What is your favorite thing to do when you are not in school?"
- "Do you like sports? What sport do you like the most?"
- "What is your favorite food? Your favorite color?"
- "If you could be any animal, what would you be?"
- "Do you have a favorite part of your school day?"
- "Tell me about your family. Do you have pets?"

Try to get students to share information about themselves, and use that information in the future as rewards or things to talk about with them. Some other ways that you can build trust and a positive relationship with a student include genuinely acknowledging the student when you see them outside the classroom, giving the student genuine positive feedback and compliments to build their self-confidence, and being transparent that you aren't perfect and make mistakes as well.

Another way to build relationships with students is to use praise statements regularly. Praise is a very effective strategy that educators can use to decrease problem behavior and increase positive behavior (Cavanaugh, 2013). Research has recommended using six praise statements every fifteen minutes to ensure that you are frequently directing students toward the positive behavior you want to see (Pisacreta, Tincani, Connell, & Axelrod, 2011). The goal is to spend more time giving students positive reinforcement for their good behaviors and choices while reducing the time you spend on their negative behaviors. You may also reach a point where there aren't positive behaviors happening to reinforce, so instead of giving attention to the negative ones, you can simply choose to ignore the behaviors altogether.

### Precorrection

Precorrection is a proactive strategy that can help with frustration tolerance. It is designed to prevent predictable problem behaviors from occurring and to increase the likelihood that expected behaviors will take place.

Here, you are focusing on behaviors that have not yet occurred during the lesson or on that day. To use precorrection with a student, you can do the following.

- Use a visual cue (such as a card, picture, or hand gesture) to remind the student of behavioral expectations.

- Remind the student about whether they are working for a reward.

- Review procedures for the task and how the student can signal if they need help.

When you are proactive and attentive to the student, you can correct many behaviors before they even happen, which will allow the student to feel successful and positive in the classroom environment.

### Proximity

Proximity involves using one's physical presence to deter undesirable behaviors. A study exploring the impact of teacher-student proximity on classroom engagement highlights the importance of physical closeness in promoting positive classroom behaviors. Its findings indicate that closer proximity between adults and students significantly increases student engagement (Dong, Liu, & Zheng, 2021). Consistent and strategic movement, particularly positioning oneself near students who exhibit behavioral challenges, has been shown to prevent 40 to 50 percent of problem behaviors while enhancing academic engagement. Implementing proximity as a corrective strategy is both simple and effective, and it fosters a supportive learning environment with minimal need for verbal interventions.

### Replacement Behaviors

Teaching students a replacement behavior for a problem behavior is a powerful strategy that improves students' problem-solving skills. The replacement behavior should be an appropriate behavior that serves the same function as the inappropriate one. For example, when a student disrespectfully refuses to do work because they are scared to be called on, you may teach them the replacement behavior of asking to work alone in the library section of the room to get their work done.

Replacement behaviors need to be within students' ability to do successfully and consistently. You should teach and practice a replacement behavior when a student is calm and rational. After teaching a replacement behavior, you must provide positive reinforcement to the student each time they use that behavior. By doing so, you will increase the likelihood that the replacement behavior will reoccur or increase over time (Hannigan & Djabrayan Hannigan, 2024).

### Redirection

Redirection is a proactive classroom management strategy that shifts a student's focus from disruptive behavior to a more appropriate activity without resorting to punishment. This technique is especially effective for students who may struggle with impulse control, emotional regulation, or attention maintenance. Rather than reprimanding a student for misbehavior, redirect them to refocus their energy in a positive way while maintaining their dignity and keeping the learning environment productive.

To implement redirection effectively, consistency is key. When students see that redirection is a standard response to off-task behavior, they become more likely to accept it without resistance. Offer clear choices that align with their interests and the classroom structure. For example, if a student is disrupting a group discussion, you might say, "I see you have a lot of energy right now. You can take a break in the reading corner, or you can help me pass out materials for the next activity. Which would you prefer?" Providing choices gives students a sense of control over their actions and makes them more likely to comply.

It's also important to anticipate pushback from some students who may argue or resist redirection. In these situations, remain calm, firm, and patient. Avoid engaging in a power struggle; instead, repeat the choices in a neutral tone without escalating the situation. If needed, give the student a few moments to process the choices before they respond. Sometimes, simply stepping away and giving them space can de-escalate resistance and help them move forward with the replacement behavior.

*Transitions*

Transitions can be challenging for students with behavior or emotional regulation issues, especially younger students. Moving from activity to activity or from outside to inside the classroom can be a trigger for these students. By being proactive, you can help students manage their behavior as they transition.

A successful way to help students transition is through direct and open communication. Let students know that the current activity will be ending soon and what they need to do to wrap it up (such as clean up, put materials away, and so on). Then, preview what the next activity will be and what they will be doing. Finally, make sure they know when the transition is going to happen and how much time they have to transition to the next activity. When you do this before a transition, students can better prepare themselves for the upcoming change and experience success when the transition occurs.

## Nonverbal and Visual Cues for Positive Behavioral Support

Nonverbal and visual cues are powerful, low-disruption tools that reinforce expectations, guide behavior, and support all students, especially those who struggle with verbal instructions, have special needs, or require additional structure. The following strategies promote consistency and calm communication without interrupting instruction or escalating situations.

### Nonverbal Gestures to Reinforce and Redirect Behavior

Nonverbal communication allows educators and paraprofessionals to redirect or support students subtly and effectively while maintaining a calm and supportive learning environment. Instead of calling out behavior, you can use gestures, facial expressions, or posture to reinforce expectations or offer encouragement. This approach is particularly effective for students who benefit more from visual processing or gestural communication than from verbal corrections.

Examples of nonverbal cues for redirection include the following.

- **Eye contact:** A neutral but direct gaze or raised eyebrow signals awareness and the expectation to refocus.
- **Head nodding or shaking:** A small nod can affirm on-task behavior, while a slight headshake can gently signal a correction.
- **Finger to lips:** This widely recognized cue reminds students to lower their voices or listen attentively without interrupting the lesson.

- **Pointing or gesturing:** Pointing to a task, schedule, or cool-down space helps students return to focus without words.

- **Hand signals:** Establish classroom-specific hand signals, such as a raised hand to request help, two fingers to take a bathroom break, or a time-out sign to indicate the need for a moment to self-regulate.

Nonverbal gestures are also a great way to reinforce positive behavior and encourage student participation. Examples of nonverbal cues for encouragement include the following.

- **Smiles:** A warm smile reassures students and builds a sense of trust, especially for those who need encouragement.

- **Thumbs-up:** A simple thumbs-up can boost students' confidence and acknowledge good work or behavior without stopping instruction.

- **Clapping or silent cheers:** For moments when verbal praise might be disruptive, a small clap, an air high five, or a celebratory fist pump can show enthusiasm and encouragement.

- **Affirmative gestures:** Nodding when a student answers a question correctly or makes a good effort reinforces their engagement and encourages continued participation.

For students who require extra support, particularly those with special needs, language barriers, or behavioral challenges, establishing personalized nonverbal signals can be highly effective. Work with students to develop cues they understand and feel comfortable with, such as a tap on the desk to signal focus, a hand over the heart to express understanding, or a subtle wave to indicate they need a break. By consistently using nonverbal cues, you can reduce disruptions, foster a positive learning environment, and communicate warmly and efficiently with all students, regardless of their learning preferences or needs.

### Visual Cues to Support Behavior and Understanding

Visual cues enhance learning and behavior management by offering concrete, accessible reminders of expectations. They provide clarity, structure, and predictability, especially for students who may struggle with impulse control, verbal communication, or solely verbal instructions. Here are some types of visual cues and how you can use them to support students.

- **Wearable visual cues:** Paraprofessionals and teachers often wear lanyards or bracelets with laminated cue cards that they can quickly point to during instruction. These visuals might include the following.

  - Behavioral expectations (such as "Raise your hand" and "Use kind words")

  - Emotional regulation strategies (such as "Take a deep breath" and "Ask for a break")

  - Social skill prompts (such as "Remember personal space" and "Take turns")

  By having these cues readily available, you can quickly redirect students by pointing to the visuals without interrupting instruction or engaging in a verbal back-and-forth.

- **Posters and wall displays:** Visual reminders posted around the classroom reinforce norms without interrupting teaching. These might include the following.

  - Picture-based classroom rules (such as photos of students raising their hands)

  - Self-regulation steps (such as "Stop, breathe, think, and choose")

  - Visual schedules that outline daily routines

  - Scenario-based expectations (such as "What does respectful listening look like?")

  While teachers typically lead the process of designing and posting classroom visuals, paraprofessionals often have meaningful input to share, especially when supporting specific students or small groups. They may suggest visuals based on student needs, help model expected behaviors for photos, or assist with maintaining or updating displays.

- **Portable visual cues:** Carrying a small folder, notebook, or flipbook of visuals allows for consistent support throughout the day and in different environments. These visual cues might include the following.

  - Behavior choice boards that let students select appropriate actions

  - Calming strategies or emotional regulation guides

  - Mini social stories showing expected behaviors

  - Visual schedules for the day

For younger students or those who have special needs or are learning English, consider using photos of students in the class that show them modeling the correct behaviors. This makes expectations more personalized and relatable.

Instead of giving a verbal reprimand, a paraprofessional can discreetly show a visual reminder to help a student get back on track. By consistently using non-verbal and visual cues, either alone or together, you will create a more inclusive, responsive, and respectful learning environment. These strategies build student independence, reduce behavioral disruptions, and foster strong, supportive connections between staff and students. All these tools prevent power struggles and empower students to self-correct with dignity.

Figure 4.2 (page 80) contains twenty-four visual cue cards that can be used as wearable cues, posters, or portable cues.

### Time-Outs and Breaks

To help students with emotional regulation, provide them with short breaks to compose themselves; you can discuss these breaks with the classroom teacher beforehand. You may even provide some students with "break cards" to take two or three breaks daily when needed. Often, the classroom has an area set up for their breaks, or you, as the paraprofessional, might take them outside for some fresh air and bring them back when they are ready. This is an easy and practical method to calm a student and redirect them back to learning.

### Modeling of Appropriate Behavior

Students' misbehaviors are often minor irritations more than anything else. They yell out, don't start their work as instructed, touch other students, get up and walk around the classroom, write on their desks, put their heads down, don't participate, and so on. These behaviors can impact teaching and learning. The trick to addressing these behaviors is not to overreact, because overreacting can cause even more disruption. Personal reactions that show a student your frustration include the following.

- Raising your voice
- Sighing loudly
- Defending yourself
- Resorting to comebacks
- Stating that you are irritated
- Grimacing or making angry facial expressions
- Getting too close to the student
- Rolling your eyes
- Crossing your arms

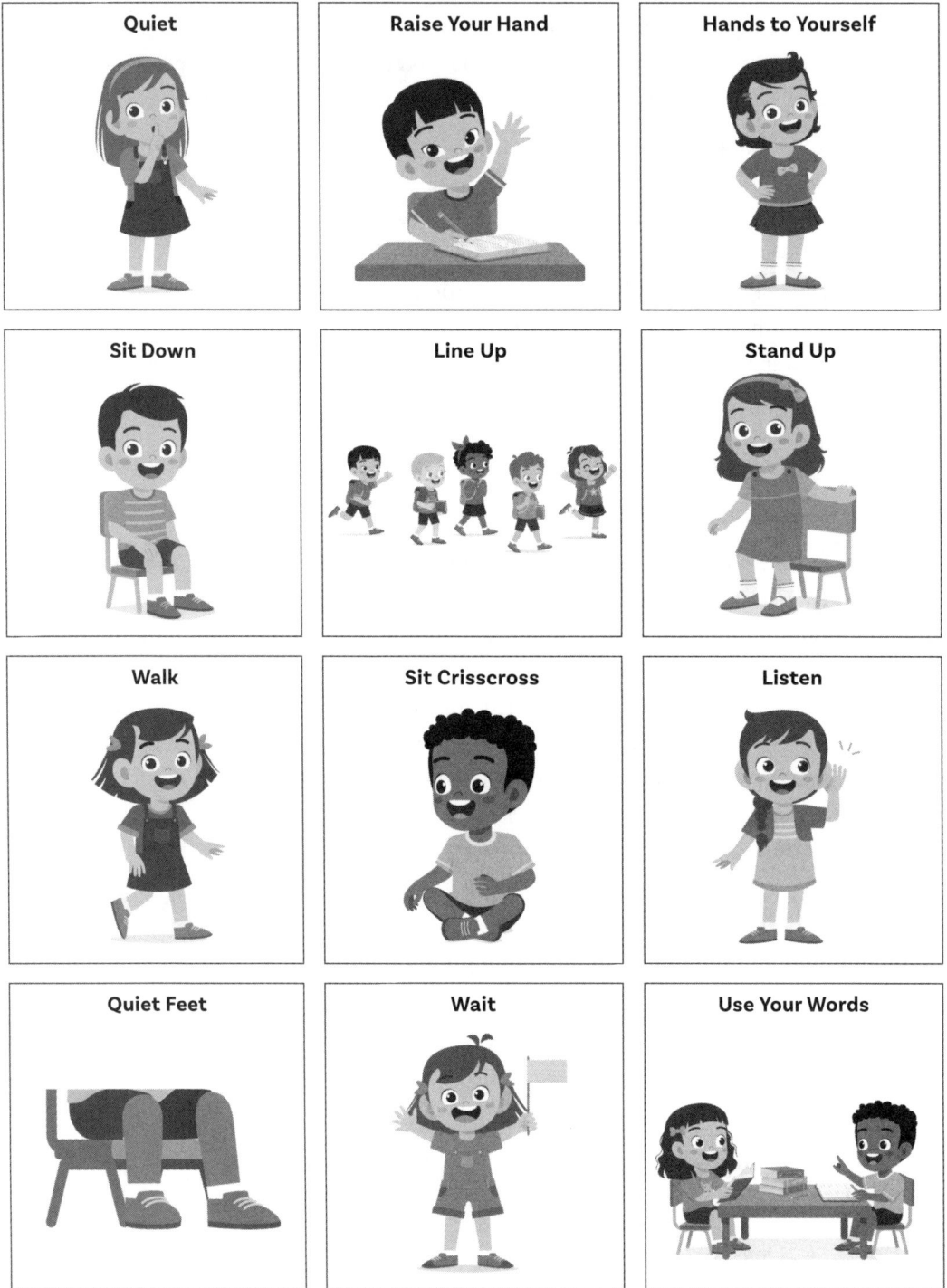

**Figure 4.2: Visual cue cards to wear, display, or carry.**

*Visit **go.SolutionTree.com/instruction** to download a free reproducible version of this figure.*

**Break Time**

**Take a Breath**

**Drink of Water**

**Snack Time**

**Stay Calm**

**Transition**

**Clean Up**

**Eyes on Teacher**

**Good Job / Thumbs-Up**

**Help**

**Bathroom**

Instead of reacting in these ways, keep calm, use a positive tone with students, and remind them of classroom expectations. When you feel yourself reacting strongly (and we all do sometimes), take time to calm yourself, even if it seems like you don't have time for that. Your behavior can affect the behavior of your students, so it is important to always be aware of how you are acting. Take some deep breaths, return to using nonverbal interventions like eye contact and gestures to redirect students, and move into closer proximity to the student. Remember, the only behavior you can control is your own.

> Remember, the only behavior you can control is your own.

We would all like to be able to snap our fingers and have students with challenging behaviors suddenly become model students. But it may take years for some students to grow into their well-behaved selves. Therefore, we have to realize that we cannot control students and force them to behave. Their behavior is not a reflection of our professional skills.

## Support for Students With Escalated Needs: De-escalation, Elopement, and Sensory Sensitivities

While you can address many behavioral challenges through proactive classroom strategies, some students require more intensive support. This section explores strategies for de-escalating upset students, responding to elopement, and managing sensory sensitivities. These skills are particularly helpful when working with students who struggle with emotional regulation, communication, or self-advocacy.

### De-escalation Strategies for Upset Students

Students may become agitated due to frustration, sensory overload, or emotional dysregulation. Recognizing early signs of agitation in students with behavioral challenges allows paraprofessionals to intervene before behaviors escalate. Agitation can manifest in various ways, such as increased restlessness, an elevated tone of voice, clenched fists, or avoidance behaviors. Agitated reactions in students can range from just being verbally upset to physically expressing strong emotions. By being attentive to these behaviors, you can proactively address the underlying causes of agitation and prevent potential outbursts.

If you are assigned to support a student who lacks emotional control and easily becomes agitated, ideally your school or district will give you specific training. When working with an agitated student, use positive and proactive strategies to de-escalate the situation. You may provide the student with a quiet space to calm down, offer sensory tools or accommodations, or use mindfulness and self-regulation techniques. Sometimes, students find themselves upset and make poor decisions based on their emotional state. When their behavior has a strong emotional component, you can help students calm down using de-escalation strategies such as the following.

- **Use breathing techniques:** Guide students through deep breathing or breathe alongside them.

- **Create a cool-down space:** Designate a calming area where students can reset.

- **Teach emotional vocabulary:** Help students name their feelings. For example, "I feel hot" might be a student's way to express anger.

- **Use physical grounding strategies:** Encourage students to place their hands in their pockets or hold their own hands to ground themselves.

- **Incorporate calming stories or books:** Use literature to help students identify with characters who are managing similar feelings.

- **Reinforce calm behavior:** Offer praise as students work through their emotions—"You're doing a great job calming yourself."

By acknowledging and accepting the student's feelings and needs, you can help the student regain control and prevent further escalation of behaviors.

If your paraprofessional assignment does not include being responsible for such a student, then you will play more of a support role if and when you are around a student who is struggling. That support role might simply mean you stay close to a fellow paraprofessional who is trying to calm a student. It might mean you talk with a student who is getting upset while their paraprofessional is on a break, and you provide calm, nonthreatening reassurance. Regardless of your role, de-escalation is a valuable skill that will strengthen your ability to effectively support all students.

### Supportive Language Techniques

You can use a calm tone of voice and thoughtful, supportive language to help soothe an upset student. The following responses are not steps that you must take in a specific order; instead, think of them as individual tools you can use on their own or in combination, depending on the situation and the student's needs.

- **Stay calm:** "I see you're feeling frustrated right now. It's OK to feel that way when something is tough."

- **Acknowledge emotions:** "It's OK to feel upset. Math can be hard sometimes, and I'm here to help."

- **Offer support:** "How about we take a short break, and then we can tackle this problem together?"

- **Simplify the task:** "Let's start with one easy problem, and then we can build up from there."

- **Praise efforts:** "I like how hard you're trying! Let's keep going step by step."

As you consistently practice these strategies, your collection of superhero tools for calming students will continue to grow.

### *Responses to Student Elopement*

If a student elopes, meaning they leave a supervised or assigned area (such as the classroom, playground, or school grounds) without permission, you must act swiftly but calmly. Your first step should always be to notify the lead teacher, the administrator, or another adult. Never attempt to manage an elopement situation entirely on your own.

Follow your school's specific elopement protocol. This may include alerting the front office or security team. If this protocol directs you to follow the student, keep a safe distance and avoid physical contact unless you have received specific training. Speak in a calm, reassuring tone and avoid using language that may escalate panic.

According to trauma-informed practice, students in distress may run away as a survival response to stress (SAMHSA, 2014). Many students elope because they are overwhelmed or in a heightened fight, flight, or freeze response. Elopement is often a form of communication. Use gentle language such as "You're safe. Let's take a walk together," or offer them a distraction. When the student is ready, help them return to a calm space.

> Students in distress may run away as a survival response to stress. Elopement is often a form of communication.

After the situation is resolved, document the incident and debrief with your classroom teacher and other relevant school personnel to understand what triggered the elopement and how to prevent future occurrences. Remember that elopement is a way that students try to communicate with us. Take time to talk with the student once they have calmed down, and try to understand what triggered them to run away. The more you learn about your student, the better you will know their triggers and how to prevent future elopements.

### Support of Sensory Sensitivities

Some students with behavioral challenges also experience sensory processing differences. They have heightened sensitivities to certain stimuli, such as loud noises, bright lights, or certain textures. These sensitivities can cause students to feel overwhelmed or agitated and to exhibit challenging behaviors such as acting out or eloping.

Begin by observing and identifying potential triggers for sensory sensitivities in students. This may involve paying attention to a student's reactions to certain stimuli or environments and seeking input from the student or their caregivers. Once you identify triggers, you can work to minimize or eliminate them in the learning environment.

Work with the teacher to provide a sensory-friendly learning environment that will make students feel more comfortable and supported. You may create a quiet space for students who are easily overwhelmed by noise, adjust the classroom lighting and layout to reduce sensory overload, use calming colors and textures, minimize distractions, and have opportunities for movement and sensory input throughout the day. Sensory accommodations may also include having sensory tools such as noise-canceling headphones, providing fidget tools for students who have trouble sitting still, or using visual schedules to help students stay organized.

Sensory breaks can also be incorporated into students' daily routines. These breaks allow students to regulate their sensory input and manage their arousal levels, which can prevent behavioral outbursts and promote focus and attention. Sensory breaks can be scheduled throughout the day or offered as needed, depending on a student's individual needs and preferences.

By creating a supportive sensory environment and giving students the breaks they need to meet their needs, you can help students with behavioral challenges feel more comfortable and engaged in the learning process. Talk with students about their sensory needs and help them become more aware of their needs and how to meet them. This will lead them to advocate for themselves and develop coping strategies for their sensory needs.

Figure 4.3 (page 86) shows an example of a sensory diet for a student who needs consistent breaks and increased sensory input.

Sensory diets combine various sensory inputs and activities to address different needs and help students stay engaged and regulated throughout the school day. You will need to find out what works best for each student you work with and allow students to be part of creating their sensory diets. For example, some students thrive with fidget gadgets, and others do not.

### Morning Routine

**Deep pressure activities (five minutes):** Begin the day by having the student squeeze a stress ball to provide them with calming proprioceptive input.

**Stretching or yoga (five minutes):** Teach the student simple stretches or yoga poses to help them with body awareness and relaxation.

### Midmorning Break

**Movement break (five minutes):** Allow the student to do jumping jacks, run in place, use a mini trampoline, or engage in other activities to get their body moving and increase their alertness.

**Fidget toys (five minutes):** Provide the student with options like fidget spinners, putty, or textured objects for tactile stimulation during quiet work periods.

### Lunchtime

**Gum or crunchy snacks:** Allow the student to chew gum or eat crunchy snacks, which can help with oral sensory needs and increase focus. Check with the classroom teacher to see if this is against any rules. Also check with the teacher on snack duration and any food restrictions.

**Calming activity (five minutes):** Before or after lunch, the student can use a calming app or listen to soothing music to help regulate their sensory systems.

### Afternoon Session

**Weighted vest or lap pad (ten minutes):** For a student who might benefit from deep pressure input, a weighted vest or lap pad can provide calming input while they are sitting at their desk.

**Sensory break stations (ten minutes):** Set up stations with different sensory activities, such as a tactile bin filled with rice or beans, a mini sandbox, and a bubble machine.

### End of the Day

**Mindfulness or breathing exercises (five minutes):** Practice deep breathing or mindfulness exercises to help the student transition out of the school day and regulate their sensory systems.

**Visual schedule review (five minutes):** Review a visual schedule or use a calm-down corner with soft lighting and calming visuals to help the student prepare for the end of the day.

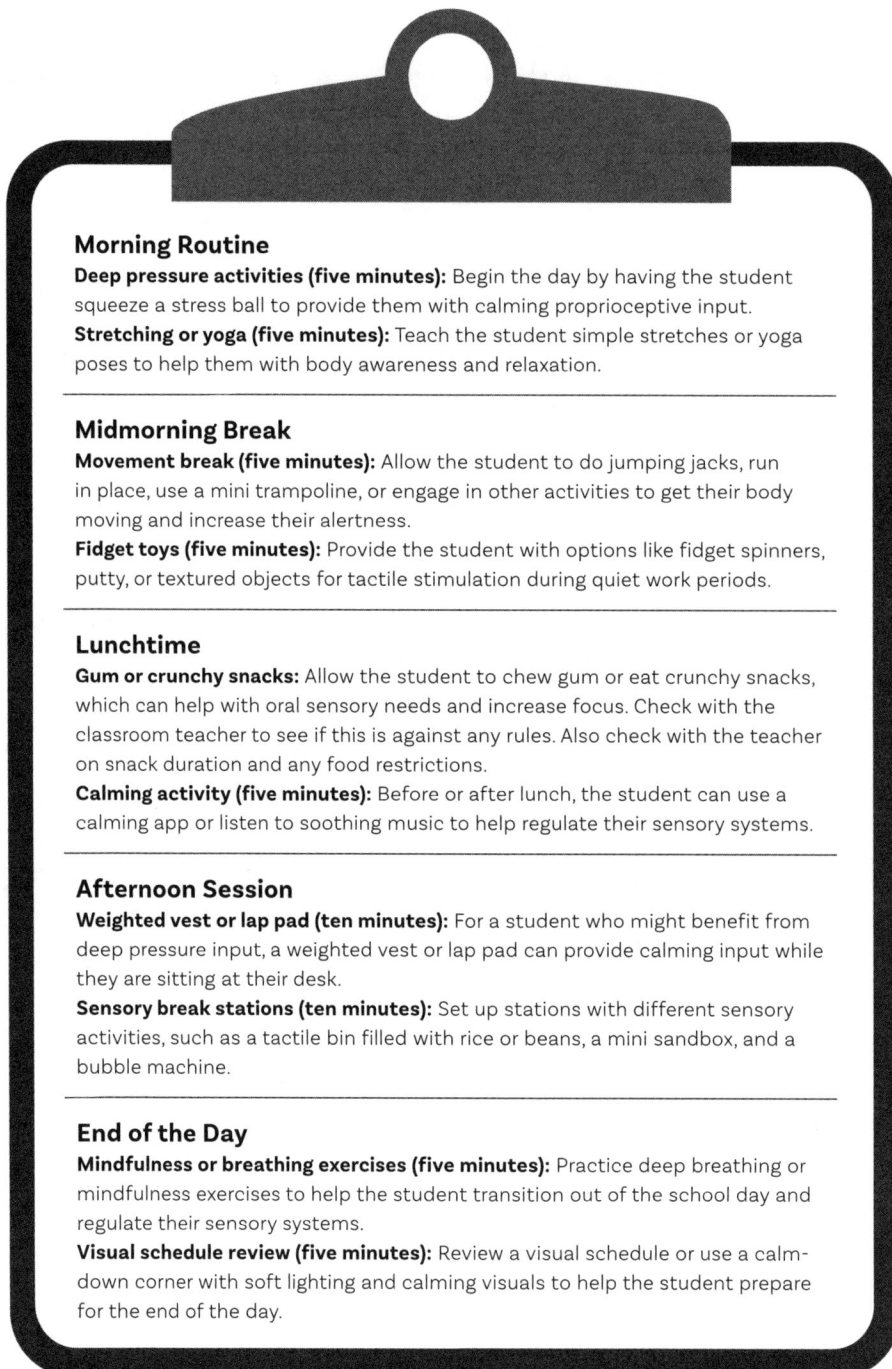

**Figure 4.3: Sample student sensory diet activities.**

## ADHD and Learning Challenges

Educators who work with students who have behavioral challenges must have a strong understanding of ADHD and other learning differences to provide effective support. This class of neurodevelopmental disorders can impact students' ability to focus, control their impulses, and regulate their behavior. Students with ADHD may struggle with staying on task, following instructions, and managing their emotions, which can lead to disruptive behaviors in the classroom. For the purposes of this section, we'll focus most explicitly on ADHD, but many other attention issues, including those without hyperactivity, also apply here.

The National Center for Biotechnology Information shares that worldwide, approximately 5 percent of the school population is diagnosed with ADHD (Jangmo et al., 2019). Research consistently shows that ADHD significantly undermines academic performance. Students with ADHD, especially those experiencing prominent inattention, tend to earn lower grades, perform worse on standardized tests, repeat grades more often, and more frequently require special education support compared to their peers (Jangmo et al., 2019). These academic struggles are largely linked to deficits in executive function, particularly working memory, planning, and impulse control, which are common to ADHD and essential for successful engagement in school tasks (Reflection Sciences, n.d.). Students with ADHD can easily become frustrated by school tasks, which leads to disruptive or attention-seeking behaviors that compound their academic challenges (Moore et al., 2018).

When working with students with ADHD, you must remember that their behaviors are not intentional disruptions but rather reflections of neurological differences. ADHD affects executive function, impulse control, and attention regulation, making it difficult for students to stay on task, follow directions, and remain engaged for long periods (CDC, 2022; DuPaul & Stoner, 2014). Your role as a paraprofessional is to provide structure, encouragement, and practical support to help them succeed. The following strategies are widely endorsed by ADHD research and classroom-based interventions (Barkley, 2013; CHADD, n.d.).

- **Create a structured environment:** A predictable and organized classroom helps students with ADHD stay focused. Clearly define areas for different activities (such as a reading corner, a quiet work zone, and a group work area) and ensure students understand where they should be at different times. Minimize clutter and distractions to create a workspace that supports concentration.

- **Use visual aids:** Visual schedules, step-by-step instructions, and classroom rules posted in an easy-to-read format can give students with ADHD the structure they need. Using visual timers or color-coded task lists can reinforce expectations and keep students on track throughout the day.

- **Break tasks into smaller steps:** Large assignments or multistep directions can be overwhelming for students with ADHD. Breaking tasks into smaller, manageable steps allows them to focus on one piece at a time and increases their chances of successfully completing the work. Providing them with checklists or graphic organizers can also help with organization.

- **Provide clear instructions:** Students with attention challenges often struggle to retain verbal instructions. Give clear, concise directions and pair them with visual or written cues when possible. It's also helpful to ask students to repeat instructions back to you to ensure they understand.

- **Use positive reinforcement:** Recognizing and rewarding positive behavior encourages students with ADHD to stay on task. Praise specific behaviors ("Great job staying in your seat during the lesson!") and consider using reward systems, such as token boards or behavior charts, to motivate students.

- **Incorporate movement breaks:** Sitting still for long periods can be challenging for students with ADHD. Allowing brief movement breaks—such as for stretching, a quick walk, or simple exercises—can help students release excess energy and refocus on their work.

- **Offer flexible seating:** Some students concentrate better when they have the option to stand, use fidget tools, or sit on wobble stools. While flexible seating can be beneficial, it's important to monitor its effectiveness, as some students may become more distracted rather than more focused.

- **Establish consistent routines and expectations:** Predictability helps students with ADHD feel secure and understand what is expected of them. Keeping daily routines consistent and giving advance notice of transitions can reduce students' anxiety and increase their ability to follow directions.

- **Use technology wisely:** Technology can be a great tool for engagement. Educational apps, interactive whiteboards, and audiobooks can provide alternative ways for students to learn. However, it's essential that you monitor technology use to ensure that students are using technology as a learning aid rather than a distraction.

- **Provide regular feedback:** Students with ADHD benefit from frequent, immediate feedback to help them stay on track. Constructive feedback should be specific and encouraging, highlighting both their strengths and their areas for improvement. Instead of saying, "Pay attention," try, "You did a great job focusing on your reading for five minutes! Let's see if we can do five more."

A positive way of viewing ADHD is that it can help students find success—especially when they learn how to channel their unique strengths. According to the ADHD Centre (2022) in the United Kingdom, having ADHD can be seen as a "superpower," and many successful people attribute their creativity, drive, and resilience to it. Traits commonly associated with ADHD, such as the following, can lead to exceptional accomplishments when paired with the right environment and support.

- **Hyperfocus:** Although individuals with ADHD often struggle to sustain attention on routine tasks, they can become intensely focused on activities that deeply interest them. This ability to lock in can result in highly productive work and deep engagement with creative or complex challenges.

- **High level of passion:** Many individuals with ADHD feel emotions intensely, which can translate into enthusiasm and passion for their interests. This emotional investment can drive them to pursue their goals wholeheartedly and inspire people around them.

- **Determination and drive:** Once they find something meaningful, students with ADHD can show remarkable perseverance. Their determination often stems from an inner desire to prove themselves, overcome obstacles, or achieve personal excellence.

- **Risk taking:** While risk taking can sometimes lead to impulsive decisions, it can also lead to innovation and bold thinking. Individuals with ADHD may be more willing to try new things, take initiative, and pursue unconventional solutions—traits often linked to entrepreneurial success.

- **Optimism:** Despite challenges, many people with ADHD maintain a positive outlook and resilience in the face of setbacks. This optimism can fuel their persistence and willingness to try again, even after failure.

- **Imagination:** ADHD is often associated with creative thinking and the ability to see connections others might miss. Students with ADHD may be especially good at thinking outside the box, generating original ideas, and approaching problems from new angles.

By viewing ADHD as a superpower and not a disability, you can help students accept how their brain works and harness it for future success. Your job is to prepare your students to experience success and enjoyment in life as they learn to harness their energy and grow in an environment of acceptance and optimism. You've got this, superhero!

## Meet Ms. Garcia: Managing Behavior for Success in the Classroom

Oliver is a fourth-grade student with a history of impulsive behavior and difficulty staying focused during class activities. His teacher has enlisted a paraprofessional, Ms. Garcia, to work with Oliver and help manage his behavior.

Let's look at some strategies Ms. Garcia uses to be a superhero paraprofessional for Oliver.

- **Building a positive relationship:** Ms. Garcia starts by creating a positive relationship with Oliver. She takes the time to learn about his interests, his preferences, and any challenges he may be facing.

- **Using visual supports:** Recognizing that Oliver responds well to visual cues, Ms. Garcia creates a visual schedule for him. The schedule outlines the day's activities and transitions, providing predictability.

- **Tracking behavioral patterns:** Ms. Garcia keeps a behavior log that the teacher asked her to use to track Oliver's behaviors. She notes when positive behaviors occur and identifies any patterns or triggers for challenging behaviors.

- **Implementing a token system:** Ms. Garcia introduces a token system where Oliver earns tokens for exhibiting positive behaviors. Once he accumulates a certain number of tokens, he can exchange them for a preferred activity or small reward.

- **Using proximity control:** Ms. Garcia strategically positions herself near Oliver during class activities to provide support and encouragement. She uses proximity control to redirect his focus when needed.

- **Incorporating breaks:** Recognizing that Oliver benefits from short breaks, Ms. Garcia works with the teacher to establish a system where he can take brief breaks in a designated area when he feels overwhelmed.

- **Developing a behavior contract:** After the teacher collaboratively develops a behavior contract with Oliver, Ms. Garcia learns about the contract and uses it to support Oliver. His contract outlines specific expectations, consequences for challenging behaviors, and rewards for meeting behavioral goals.

- **Collaborating with other professionals:** Ms. Garcia regularly communicates with the teacher and the school counselor to share insights and discuss strategies for consistent support for Oliver.

- **Celebrating small achievements:** By celebrating small achievements and positive behaviors, Ms. Garcia acknowledges Oliver's efforts and progress and fosters a sense of accomplishment.

- **Modeling positive social interactions:** Ms. Garcia models appropriate behavior and encourages positive interactions with peers, reinforcing social skills in real-life situations.

By consistently using these strategies and a collaborative approach involving the teacher and other professionals, Ms. Garcia provides Oliver with the support he needs to succeed in the classroom while she addresses his behavioral challenges.

## Wrap-Up

This chapter discussed a critical aspect of working with students: behavioral issues. Now that you know the most common behavioral issues in classrooms, how to de-escalate upset students, and positive strategies to work with challenging students, you are well on your way to mastering this challenging aspect of working with students. In the feature box that follows, you'll find practical advice from experienced paraprofessionals who work with challenging students. Their insights are grounded in day-to-day experience. Then, in the "Notes and Reflections: Supporting Students With Behavioral and Attention Challenges" reproducible (page 93), you'll have the opportunity to thoughtfully reflect on what you've learned and consider how these insights apply to your own practice.

## *Advice From*
### SUPERHERO PARAPROFESSIONALS

"Working with students who have challenging behaviors, in both special and general education settings, can be very difficult but also very rewarding. Every student is different, so it takes patience and flexibility to determine what works for each case. At times, it can be completely draining, but even the smallest wins make it all worth it. It's about building rapport and trust, celebrating the small steps, and knowing that every bit of progress matters."

(K. Fitzsimmons, personal communication, November 6, 2024)

"I always believe building rapport and positive relationships with students is the key to dealing with behaviors. All behaviors are a form of communication. Each child communicates differently, so the child will buy into strategies that are put in place if there is trust. The job is not always easy, but making a difference to a child is worth it!"

(D. Schooler, personal communication, November 5, 2024)

"Before we can address behavior, it is crucial to establish rapport with the student. Once that relationship is established, we can address the function of the behavior. The team can implement strategies to create more appropriate replacement behaviors and increase the likelihood of those target behaviors through positive reinforcement. Progress may be slow, but we must celebrate each and every small victory!"

(C. Morand, personal communication, November 5, 2024)

# Notes and Reflections: Supporting Students With Behavioral and Attention Challenges

Take a few moments to reflect on the following questions about being a superhero paraprofessional.

1. Reflect on your own experiences with students who display challenging behaviors. How can you improve your approach to building relationships with them and identifying underlying needs?

2. What proactive strategies could you implement, and what specific examples of positive reinforcement could you use?

3. How can you create a consistent and structured environment with clear expectations for behavior?

4. What de-escalation techniques could you use if you saw a student who was upset?

5. How can you strengthen your communication and collaboration with others to better support struggling students?

# Championing Social-Emotional Well-Being

There has been a noticeable increase in the number of students coming to classrooms with anxiety, depression, and other mental health needs. One in five children and teenagers in the United States show symptoms of a mental health disorder (CDC, 2025). The most common mental health diagnoses in children and teens, according to the CDC, are depression (3.2 percent), anxiety (7.1 percent), behavior problems (7.4 percent), and ADHD (9.4 percent).

Social and emotional development in students has a direct impact on their ability to learn academically and thrive socially (Balfanz & Byrnes, 2021; Cipriano et al., 2023). Research shows that mental well-being is crucial for students' overall success and happiness (Goodwin & Long, 2022). Students who have strong mental health do better in school and are generally happier and more content than students who suffer from mental health challenges. Helping students

## KEY POINTS

- Recognize social-emotional well-being as a top priority for students.
- Help students who suffer from mental health challenges.
- Provide meaningful social-emotional learning opportunities for students.
- Teach emotional regulation.
- Work with students and their social skills.

acquire strong mental health and wellness skills goes hand in hand with academic performance and future success (Moya et al., 2022).

As a paraprofessional, you can play a vital role in addressing mental and social-emotional health in the classroom and supporting struggling students. By prioritizing their mental health and well-being, you will ensure that students improve their social skills, focus better, and enhance their learning capacities.

## The Most Common Student Mental Health Challenges

According to the CDC (2025), today's children and teens commonly face the following mental health challenges.

- **Anxiety disorders:** *Anxiety* is a term used to describe a feeling of extreme uneasiness and worry. Anxiety is a natural response for many of us when we are worrying about something. Yet if anxiety lasts a long time and prevents a student from doing typical activities, then their anxiety is not considered normal, and they may be diagnosed with an anxiety disorder.

   Some symptoms of anxiety include:

   - Stomachaches or headaches
   - Trouble sleeping
   - Lack of appetite
   - Fear of being alone or sleeping alone
   - Fear of social situations and places with a lot of people
   - Tantrums and crying in social situations
   - Restlessness
   - Problems concentrating
   - Constant worrying

   Anxiety can disrupt essential cognitive processes involved in learning. Elevated anxiety levels can impair concentration, working memory, and information processing and decrease academic performance. This disruption can lead to difficulties in absorbing and retaining new information, further hindering academic success (McCurdy et al., 2023). For instance, a study highlights that anxiety and depression symptoms may leave students at risk for lower academic scores, particularly in spelling and mathematics (McCurdy et al., 2023).

- **Depression:** Persistent feelings of sadness, hopelessness, and a lack of interest in activities are hallmark symptoms of depression, which can significantly impact students' energy levels and engagement in learning. Research indicates that depression is associated with decreased academic performance, as affected students often struggle with concentration, motivation, and participation in educational activities. For instance, a study examining the relationship between depression symptoms and academic achievement shows that students experiencing higher levels of depression have lower academic success (Wagner et al., 2022).

- **Attention-Deficit/Hyperactivity Disorder (ADHD):** While ADHD is often viewed primarily through the lens of academic difficulties, it also significantly affects a student's social-emotional well-being. Many students with ADHD struggle with emotional regulation, which can lead to frequent frustration, outbursts, or difficulty coping with everyday stressors. In fact, students with ADHD are at a higher risk of developing co-occurring conditions such as anxiety, depression, and oppositional defiant disorder (Bunford, Evans, & Wymbs, 2015). These layered challenges can intensify feelings of isolation, reduce self-esteem, and make it harder for students to build and maintain friendships. By understanding ADHD as both a learning condition and a mental health condition, educators and paraprofessionals can better support students in developing emotional awareness, self-regulation strategies, and a sense of belonging at school.

- **Behavioral disorders:** Oppositional defiant disorder and conduct disorder are behavioral disorders in children and adolescents that can lead to disruptive behaviors, defiance, and difficulty following rules. Oppositional defiant disorder is characterized by a persistent pattern of uncooperative, defiant, and hostile behavior toward authority figures, including parents and teachers, and peers. Oppositional defiant disorder can manifest with frequent temper loss, argumentativeness, deliberate annoyance of others, and refusal to comply with rules or requests (Johns Hopkins Medicine, n.d.).

- **Eating disorders:** Eating disorders, including anorexia nervosa, bulimia nervosa, and binge-eating disorder, significantly affect students' physical and emotional well-being. Physically, these disorders can lead to severe health complications such as malnutrition, electrolyte imbalances, and gastrointestinal issues, which may impair cognitive functions essential for academic success. Emotionally, students may experience heightened levels of anxiety, depression, and social withdrawal, further hindering their educational performance and personal development (American Academy of Pediatrics, 2022).

- **Substance abuse:** Student struggles with substance abuse lead to academic and behavioral issues. According to the CDC (2020), approximately two-thirds of students have tried alcohol by grade 12, and half of high schoolers claim to have used marijuana. About two in ten high school seniors claim to have used prescription medications without a prescription. It is obviously hard to learn when students' physical bodies are processing toxins and drugs.

- **Self-harm:** Self-harm, particularly among adolescents and young adults, is a significant concern in educational settings. Research indicates that students may engage in self-injurious behaviors, such as cutting, as a coping mechanism to manage overwhelming emotional distress and feelings of emptiness or to try to control their lives and environment. A study published in the *Journal of the American Academy of Child and Adolescent Psychiatry* finds that approximately 17 percent of adolescents have engaged in nonsuicidal self-injury at least once (Apter, 2014). Factors contributing to these behaviors include psychological conditions like depression and anxiety, experiences of trauma or abuse, and difficulties in interpersonal relationships. Early identification and intervention are crucial, as timely support can improve outcomes and help students manage both the physical and emotional challenges associated with self-harm.

Each of these mental health challenges, whether rooted in anxiety, depression, behavioral disorders, or other concerns, can significantly disrupt a student's ability to build positive relationships, regulate their emotions, and develop a strong sense of self. Social-emotional well-being is the foundation of learning, yet students with persistent mental health conditions may feel isolated, misunderstood, or disconnected from their peers and teachers. These difficulties can lead to low self-esteem, reduced motivation, avoidance behaviors, and challenges in developing empathy or collaboration skills. Addressing mental health needs through early identification, inclusive support systems, and trauma-informed practices is essential not only for having academic success but also for thriving socially and emotionally in school and beyond.

## Manifestation of Behaviors and Outbursts

Social-emotional and mental health challenges can manifest in various ways in the school environment. Recognizing these signs is the first step to providing effective support. The common behavioral issues discussed in chapter 4, such as defiance, off-task behavior, and attention seeking, are often rooted in skill deficits or developmental immaturity. In contrast, the behaviors described here may signal emotional distress or underlying mental health conditions that require a more sensitive, trauma-informed approach. These manifestations are often more persistent, intense, or emotionally driven, and they may not respond to standard behavioral interventions alone.

Social-emotional challenges may appear in a classroom setting in the following ways.

- **Aggressive and disruptive behaviors:** Students may exhibit aggression (hitting, yelling, or pushing) or controlling behavior (dominating or interrupting conversations) as an expression of internal turmoil, not just a desire for attention or defiance. Unlike more common disruptive behaviors, these may escalate quickly or appear disproportionate to the situation; they are often tied to anxiety, trauma, or a need for emotional control in uncertain environments.

- **Withdrawal:** While some students may be quiet or appear disengaged due to their personality or learning style, withdrawal caused by emotional distress includes active avoidance behaviors like sitting alone, refusing to speak, or showing signs of detachment or exhaustion. These behaviors are not simply indicative of inattentiveness; they reflect a deeper sense of fear, sadness, or isolation.

- **Academic challenges:** Unlike the task avoidance seen in some students with executive function difficulties, students experiencing mental health challenges may avoid work due to anxiety, intrusive thoughts, or perfectionism. Their inability to focus is often driven by internal emotional conflict rather than disinterest or a lack of understanding.

- **Physical ailments:** In chapter 4, hyperactivity or fidgeting was noted as a common behavioral pattern. However, in this context, physical symptoms such as headaches, stomachaches, or panic responses may be somatic expressions of anxiety or emotional overload. Students who have these symptoms may truly not feel well due to stress.

- **Mood swings:** Emotional volatility in students with mental health struggles differs from momentary frustration or minor defiance. These mood swings can be abrupt and intense, indicating difficulty with emotional regulation or underlying depression or trauma. What appears to be an overreaction may, in fact, be a coping response to overwhelming feelings.

- **Poor social skills:** Unlike typical developmental conflicts over sharing or turn taking, social struggles tied to mental health may include extreme sensitivity, isolation, or volatile peer interactions. Students' social withdrawal or overdependence may reflect deeper insecurity or anxiety rather than simple immaturity.

This framing helps educators recognize when a student's behavior might be signaling something more complex than surface-level misbehavior. It also supports a shift from discipline-first responses to more empathetic, individualized interventions.

Research underscores the importance of addressing these challenges. A study published in *Child Development* confirms that students who participate in social-emotional learning programs (also called *life-skills programs*) demonstrate increased academic achievement and improved social and emotional skills. These programs also lead to better attendance and engagement in learning, highlighting the positive impact of life-skills education on student well-being and academic success (Greenberg, 2023). If given the right support and therapy, students can find a new way forward in their lives and can exhibit stronger characteristics as time goes by.

## Post-Traumatic Stress Disorder

Exposure to trauma can result in symptoms of post-traumatic stress disorder, such as flashbacks, nightmares, and hypervigilance. It can lead to anxiety, irrational fears, sleep issues, anger, poor attendance, and a lack of interest in everyday activities (American Psychological Association, 2011). Schools are seeing an increase in students who have faced traumatic experiences, including the COVID-19 pandemic, natural disasters, and domestic violence. According to the umbrella review "Shadows of Trauma" (Tamir, Tekeba, Mekonen, Gebrehana, & Zegeye, 2025), the pooled prevalence of post-traumatic stress disorder among children and adolescents is approximately 25 percent.

> It is essential to recognize that students may be acting out due to past traumatic experiences rather than simply being "difficult" or "disruptive."

Educators and paraprofessionals who work with students who have behavioral or social-emotional challenges must understand trauma's impact on behavior. Trauma can manifest in various ways, including aggression, withdrawal, or emotional dysregulation. It is essential to recognize that students may be acting out due to past traumatic experiences rather than simply being "difficult" or "disruptive."

Many students come to school having experienced adverse childhood experiences. Also, approximately 64 percent of U.S. adults have experienced at least one type of adverse childhood experience, which can have adverse effects on their mental and emotional health (Swedo et al., 2023). The most common adverse childhood experiences include the following (Merrick et al., 2019).

- Divorce of parents
- Incarceration of a relative
- Mental illness in the family
- Death of a loved one
- Physical or emotional abuse
- Mother experiencing violence
- Physical or emotional neglect

Traumatic experiences can include a wide range of events that some people might not consider traumatic. Whatever its significance, trauma can leave a lasting imprint because children rely on adults to keep them safe. Once a student has experienced trauma, they may show behavioral and physical reactions, such as difficulty sleeping or eating, emotional dysregulation, anger, anxiety, or withdrawal. They may also develop somatization, where emotional distress manifests as physical symptoms of discomfort, like headaches or stomachaches, without recognition of the emotional root (Kroska, Roche, & O'Hara, 2018; Malesu, 2024).

Working with students who have experienced trauma can be challenging; however, many students will find a way to adapt and learn from their experiences with the right support and understanding, leading to post-traumatic growth. *Post-traumatic growth* refers to the positive psychological changes that can occur following exposure to traumatic events. These changes may include enhanced personal strength, improved relationships, and greater appreciation for life. Researchers examined this growth in children exposed to both traumatic and nontraumatic but seriously upsetting events. These researchers used the Posttraumatic Growth Inventory for Children-Revised (PTGI-C-R) to assess growth across five domains: (1) new possibilities, (2) relating to others, (3) personal strength, (4) spiritual change, and (5) appreciation of life. Their findings indicate that children can experience post-traumatic growth across all these areas. This study highlights the importance of supportive interventions for creating positive psychological transformations in young individuals facing adversity (Laceulle, Kleber, & Alisic, 2015).

## Help With Mental Health Challenges

Teaching students social skills and working with them to strengthen their emotional development have been shown to reduce anxiety, suicidal thoughts, depression, and impulsive behaviors and assist with trauma-related challenges (Taylor, Oberle, Durlak, & Weissberg, 2017). In addition, working with students on their overall wellness skills improves their self-care, peer interactions, attendance, behavior, and academic performance (DePaoli, Atwell, & Bridgeland, 2017). Being the superhero you are, you will want to be part of this fantastic work by employing various social-emotional strategies to support students with social-emotional needs. Here are some good starting places.

- **Use a strength-based approach:** When you work with a student who needs additional social-emotional support, begin with what the student is already strong in. Think of yourself as a "strength spotter." Focusing on what they can already do well shows the student that you value them for who they are and for their skills. Many students with mental health challenges are not even aware of their positive traits. Pointing out those areas and complementing their strengths provides an excellent foundation for them to grow. It also helps us as adults not focus too much on the negative behaviors or challenges and recognize the skills and strengths of each child. This strength spotting isn't just for students; it is also for yourself, because you need to know your strengths and skills as a person and a paraprofessional. What are five strengths you have?

- **Help create a safe and supportive environment:** Creating a safe and supportive environment is essential when working with students with social-emotional challenges. Work with the classroom teacher to intentionally create a positive environment for your students to thrive in. This could mean the classroom is warm and well organized, and when students arrive, they know there are structures and routines in place that will keep them safe. The physical environment might also include centers and areas for students to take breaks if needed. Just by being aware of the physical environment and keeping it orderly and safe, you are helping students feel cared for.

  Let's say Ms. Lee, a paraprofessional in a second-grade classroom, notices that one of her students, Daniel, becomes overwhelmed by loud noises and crowded spaces. To support him, she collaborates with the teacher to set up a quiet corner in the classroom with noise-canceling headphones, fidget tools, and a visual timer. Over time, Daniel learns to recognize when he needs a break and effectively uses the space to self-regulate. This leads to fewer disruptions and increased engagement in learning activities.

- **Build relationships with students:** Building positive and trusting relationships with students is the foundation of effective support. It involves understanding students individually and gaining insights into their interests, strengths, and challenges. By taking a personalized approach, you create an environment where students feel valued and supported. This connection lays the groundwork for meaningful interactions and allows you to tailor your support to the unique needs of each student.

Establishing such relationships fosters a positive learning atmosphere and contributes to students' well-being and academic success under your care. For example, Mr. Johnson, a paraprofessional in a fifth-grade classroom, notices that a student, Lily, struggles with self-confidence and rarely participates in class discussions. He takes the time to learn about her interests and discovers she loves drawing. By incorporating art-related activities into their interactions, he builds a connection with Lily and gradually encourages her to express herself more in class. Over time, she becomes more comfortable speaking up, knowing she has a supportive and understanding adult in the classroom.

- **Practicing active listening:** Practicing active listening skills is a crucial strategy for you to demonstrate empathy and understanding toward students. Actively listening to students, which involves hearing the words spoken and understanding their emotions and context, makes students feel heard and valued. Additionally, validating students' feelings is essential in acknowledging the legitimacy of their emotions. You can also provide a safe space for students to express themselves without judgment, communicate openly, and build trusting relationships.

- **Use positive reinforcement:** You play an important role in fostering a positive and supportive classroom environment by implementing strategies that reinforce positive behavior. Celebrating small successes and progress creates a culture of positivity and motivates students to engage actively in their learning journeys. By reinforcing positive behavior, you help build students' self-esteem and confidence, and you contribute to a classroom atmosphere conducive to growth and success. This emphasis on recognizing and celebrating achievements, no matter how small, fosters a sense of accomplishment and creates a foundation for continued positive engagement within the learning community.

For example, a paraprofessional working with a student who struggles with attention and on-task behavior and has frequent crying episodes might implement a sticker chart where the student earns a sticker for every ten minutes of focused work. Once the student earns five stickers, they receive a small reward, such as extra time with a preferred activity.

This system not only reinforces positive behavior but also helps the student develop self-motivation and a sense of achievement.

- **Offer choices:** Many students who have experienced trauma feel vulnerable and not in control. Offer frequent decisions and opportunities for students to feel in control of their own lives. Also, learn individual triggers that cause a student to feel unsafe and react. Once you identify these triggers, avoid these situations so that the student does not experience any other trauma-like symptoms. Let's say a student named Sam becomes very agitated when the teacher calls on students to share answers aloud in front of the class. This trigger stems from previous experiences in past schools where classmates ridiculed Sam for giving incorrect answers, causing him to feel embarrassed and anxious. After speaking with Sam and observing his behavior, the teacher learns that Sam is triggered by a fear of being judged by his peers. To avoid this trigger, the teacher starts offering Sam the opportunity to privately answer questions or write his responses on a whiteboard or paper that is not immediately visible to the rest of the class.

- **Offer frequent validation:** Validate students' feelings and offer support without judgment. When you create a supportive and nonjudgmental environment, students are more likely to open up about their mental health challenges and seek help when needed. It is also wise to first seek to understand a student before demanding that they know what is being asked of them. For instance, if a student is visibly upset and refuses to participate in class, you might calmly acknowledge their emotions by saying, "I can see you're having a tough time right now. Would you like to take a moment to breathe or talk about what's on your mind?" instead of immediately insisting that they follow instructions. This supportive approach not only validates their feelings but also opens the door for communication and creates a sense of safety to express their struggles and collaboratively find a solution.

- **Teach self-management and relationship skills:** Teach students skills such as self-awareness, self-management, social awareness, relationship skills, and responsible decision making. Let's say a student, Emily, frequently becomes upset when things don't go as planned, especially when she gets a test question wrong or doesn't finish an assignment on time. This frustration can lead to outbursts, which make it hard for her to stay focused and calm. You and the teacher begin by teaching Emily to recognize and label her emotions. The teacher introduces an emotion chart with faces representing different feelings (like happy, frustrated, sad, proud, and angry) and asks Emily to choose how she's feeling at different times during the day. You ask her how she is feeling and if she is frustrated. To help Emily manage her frustration, the teacher and you introduce strategies such as deep breathing and positive self-talk. The teacher teaches Emily to use a calm-down card with steps like "Take three deep breaths," "Think about something that makes you happy," and "Tell yourself, 'I can try again.'"

## Life-Skills Learning

To foster students' social-emotional well-being, you should implement strategies that contribute to emotional recognition and regulation. Teaching students techniques for identifying and managing their emotions empowers them with valuable skills for navigating various situations. You can contribute to their emotional intelligence by creating a supportive environment where students can learn to express themselves in healthy and adaptive ways. Model healthy emotional expression and coping mechanisms as tangible examples of how students can constructively handle their feelings.

Some educators use social-emotional learning or life-skills programs and activities to promote students' awareness of their emotions and how those emotions can affect their learning. Research shows that students who participate in these lessons and activities do better academically, have less anxiety, are less aggressive with their peers, and pay better attention in the classroom. The effects are largest for students who are at risk academically and behaviorally (Hagelskamp, Brackett, Rivers, & Salovey, 2013).

A well-known framework for this type of support in the classroom was created by the Collaborative for Academic, Social, and Emotional Learning (CASEL, n.d.). The CASEL (n.d.) framework focuses on five primary skills that students must learn to help them with their performance in the classroom and their overall emotional wellness.

1. **Self-awareness:** The ability to recognize and understand one's own emotions, thoughts, and values and how they influence behavior; self-awareness also includes accurately assessing one's strengths and weaknesses, leading to a well-grounded sense of confidence and purpose.

2. **Self-management:** The ability to regulate emotions, thoughts, and behaviors effectively in different situations; this includes managing

stress, controlling impulses, and motivating oneself to achieve personal and academic goals.

3. **Responsible decision making:** The capacity to make thoughtful, ethical, and constructive choices about personal and social behavior; it involves considering the well-being of oneself and others as one evaluates the consequences of their actions and makes decisions based on social norms and safety.

4. **Relationship skills:** Establishing and maintaining healthy, rewarding relationships through effective communication, active listening, cooperation, and conflict resolution; it also includes the ability to seek and offer help when needed.

5. **Social awareness:** Being able to empathize with others from diverse backgrounds and cultures; it includes understanding social norms for behavior and being able to recognize family, school, and community resources and supports.

The CASEL (n.d.) framework is founded on the idea that the adults in a school must work together to provide ongoing instruction and support in these five areas. With this in mind, these adults also need to be strong in these five areas so they can always model them. You, as a paraprofessional, will help model the five skills and teach them to students (Frey et al., 2022). In *The Social-Emotional Learning Playbook: A Guide to Student and Teacher Well-Being*, authors Nancy Frey, Douglas Fisher, and Dominique Smith (2022) share research that shows how prioritizing social-emotional health decreases adults' stress levels and increases how much they enjoy their jobs. Therefore, prioritizing your social-emotional health is of utmost importance.

Other programs that address social-emotional education include the following.

- **Second Step (www.secondstep.org):** Developed by Committee for Children, Second Step provides age-appropriate lessons and activities to help students build social-emotional skills. It covers topics such as empathy, emotion management, and problem solving.

- **RULER (https://rulerapproach.org):** Developed by the Yale Center for Emotional Intelligence, *RULER* stands for *recognizing, understanding, labeling, expressing,* and *regulating* emotions. This approach integrates emotional intelligence into the curriculum to help create a positive emotional climate in schools.

- **Zones of Regulation (https://zonesofregulation.com):** Developed by Leah M. Kuypers, this program focuses on self-regulation and emotional control. It categorizes emotions into different zones to help students appropriately identify and manage their feelings.

- **MindUP (www.mindup.org):** Developed by the Goldie Hawn Foundation, MindUP teaches students about neuroscience, mindfulness, and positive psychology. It includes activities and lessons to promote emotional well-being and focused attention.

- **Promoting Alternative Thinking Strategies (PATHS; www.emozi.net):** Developed by the Channing Bete Company, PATHS enhances emotional understanding and reduces aggression and behavior problems. It emphasizes teaching problem-solving and social skills.

- **Open Circle (www.open-circle.org):** Developed by Pamela Seigle, Open Circle focuses on creating positive school climates. It includes lessons on communication, problem solving, and community building.

## Strategies for Teaching Emotional Regulation

Teachers and paraprofessionals are vital in ensuring students develop the necessary skills to navigate social interactions and regulate their emotions. Sometimes, students (and adults) simply do not know what they are feeling or how to handle their feelings once they gain awareness. Because feelings can drive impulsive behaviors, it is important to include intentional instruction in emotional regulation in any behavior program. By empowering students to build positive connections with others and manage their behavior, you are helping them gain lifelong skills.

Developing social skills and emotional regulation is essential for students' success in school and beyond. Many students, particularly those with disabilities, need extra support in understanding their emotions, recognizing social cues, and managing their responses. Here are some effective strategies to foster these skills (CASEL, 2023; Elbertson, Jennings, & Brackett, 2025).

- **Emotion identification:** Before students can regulate their emotions, they need to recognize and label them. Tools such as emotion charts with pictures of facial expressions or activities like emotion charades can help students connect feelings to words (CASEL, 2023). Storybooks and guided discussions are especially effective for younger students in modeling safe and relatable emotional experiences (Denham, Bassett, & Wyatt, 2015).

- **Awareness building through body cues:** Many students struggle to recognize the physical signs of their emotions, which can make self-regulation challenging. Helping students recognize physical signs of emotions, such as a tight chest, clenched fists, or shaky hands, can provide an early warning system for self-regulation. Research shows that increasing students' awareness of their internal body systems (interoceptive awareness) helps students identify and manage their emotional states (Price & Hooven, 2018). Guided discussions, visuals, and mindfulness activities can empower students to identify and respond to body cues before their emotions escalate. Encouraging them to verbalize what they're feeling and pairing these cues with coping strategies can further strengthen their ability to self-regulate.

- **Calming techniques:** Deep breathing exercises are simple yet powerful ways to help students calm down in the moment. Techniques such as balloon breathing (where students pretend to inflate a balloon with deep breaths) or five-finger breathing (where they trace their fingers while inhaling and exhaling) are concrete, developmentally appropriate techniques for managing stress and building a habit of calming down before reacting (Schonert-Reichl & Roeser, 2016). Regular practice helps these techniques become second nature so that students can easily access them during moments of frustration or anxiety.

- **Healthy outlets:** Teaching students to channel their emotions into positive activities can give them a sense of control and self-regulation. Physical activities like stretching, jumping, or squeezing a stress ball can release frustration, while creative outlets such as drawing, journaling, or playing with clay allow students to process their emotions in constructive ways. Additionally, encouraging open communication and providing a safe space for students to express their feelings help them build emotional awareness and confidence in seeking support when needed. These methods are part of many trauma-informed and life-skills frameworks and are especially effective for students who have difficulty verbalizing emotions (Perry & Szalavitz, 2017).

- **Positive coping options for problem solving:** Many students struggle with problem solving in emotionally charged situations. Role-playing common scenarios, such as dealing with a disagreement or handling disappointment, lets students practice responding appropriately. Teaching students simple problem-solving steps like identifying the problem, thinking of solutions, and choosing a plan gives them a structured approach to resolving conflicts and making thoughtful decisions. This kind of intentional problem-solving instruction enhances self-regulation and supports students in emotionally charged or challenging situations (Better Kid Care, 2024).

- **Self-talk for emotional regulation:** Students often have negative thoughts that influence their emotions and behavior. Teaching them to use positive self-talk can reframe their thinking. For example, instead of "I can't do this," they can say, "I'll try my best." *I can* statements like "I feel frustrated, but I can take a deep breath" help students take ownership of their emotions while practicing constructive responses. Over time, developing a habit of positive self-talk can build students' resilience and improve their self-confidence (Orvell, Kross, & Gelman, 2020).

As students learn to recognize and regulate their emotions, they will be better able to socialize with others. For example, sometimes, students will exclude or not want to play with a peer who has behavioral or emotional regulation issues. By working with students to improve their emotional regulation, you will empower them to interact with others in a more effective way and form strong, positive peer relationships.

### Practicing Mindfulness

Using mindfulness with your students on a regular basis promotes calmness. Mindfulness allows you to practice being aware of your thoughts, feelings, and bodily sensations and the surrounding environment. It involves being fully present in the moment, without distractions or overwhelming reactions to what's happening. Mindfulness has been shown to reduce stress, improve focus, and enhance emotional regulation by encouraging practitioners to observe personal experiences with openness and acceptance.

Teaching students to be mindful, slow down, and breathe helps them better recognize their emotions and thoughts. It improves their emotional regulation and self-awareness, and it helps them manage stress, anxiety, and depression by focusing on the present moment and cultivating a sense of calm and clarity. By practicing mindfulness, students learn to better understand the triggers that lead to negative behaviors. Mindfulness also enhances students' overall well-being and academic performance, as students can focus their attention, manage their emotions, and approach challenges with a positive mindset (Gerszberg, n.d.).

Another helpful strategy aligned with mindfulness is teaching students to use metacognitive tools, such as the SELf-questioning method outlined in *The Metacognitive*

*Student* (Cohen, Opatosky, Savage, Stevens, & Darrah, 2021). This method encourages students to pause and ask themselves reflective questions like:

- "What am I feeling right now?"
- "What triggered that feeling?"
- "What can I do to calm myself down and refocus?"

When practiced regularly, this kind of self-questioning builds emotional intelligence and supports mindful problem solving. It empowers students to respond to challenges thoughtfully rather than react impulsively.

Mindful classroom resources and activities are readily available online, and many include videos and music that help students calm down, breathe deeply, and focus on their current feelings. If you're interested in bringing mindfulness into your daily routine, talk with your classroom teacher about what fits the students' needs and schedule. Small, consistent mindfulness practices can make a meaningful difference in your students' ability to self-regulate, build resilience, and thrive in the classroom environment.

### Learning Self-Control

Once they begin recognizing and discussing emotions, students can learn skills to address certain strong emotions, like anger and frustration. Helping students realize that they are experiencing "big feelings," or feeling angry, can lead them to identify what caused the anger. This goes a long way toward managing and controlling those emotions.

Students can learn to express their anger in calm ways, such as by saying, "I am angry because . . ." Students can also make a list of activities for dealing with their anger, like the following.

- Counting to ten slowly before saying or doing anything
- Engaging in deep breathing or other mindfulness activities
- Taking a walk or getting some type of exercise
- Writing in a journal
- Speaking to a counselor at school
- Taking a break in a break area already designated for the student

Students can come up with their own option menu by talking with you and the classroom teacher. Then, when they are angry or emotional, you can pull out their menu and allow them to decide how they want to address their emotions.

Another good idea is for you or the classroom teacher to model getting angry and then calming yourself down, or to talk to the student about something that happened to you that made you very angry and how you dealt with it. Anger is part of everyday life; normalizing it is good.

As students experience their emotions, label them, and then positively deal with them, their confidence and resilience will grow. They can get through challenging moments and control their emotions and responses. This process takes time, but by finding safe adults like you to interact with and experience success in school, students will realize that they can function and succeed in the school environment. Your role as a paraprofessional is vital, and your efforts can help students navigate challenges and succeed in school and beyond.

### *Regulating Emotions*

Students struggling with their social-emotional health are greatly confused by the power of their emotions and find it hard even to identify what they are feeling at any given moment. The Zones of Regulation is a powerful program that helps students identify and express their feelings using colors (Kuypers, 2011).

- **Blue zone:** Feelings of sickness, fatigue, or boredom
- **Green zone:** Feelings of happiness, calmness, or readiness to learn
- **Yellow zone:** Feelings of frustration, worry, or excitement
- **Red zone:** Feelings of anger or high frustration that lead to poor choices

When you teach students about the zones, they learn that emotions are normal, that everyone has them, and that these feelings have names. Also, when you teach students to recognize that they are in the red zone, they learn strategies to get out of that zone. As a paraprofessional, you can ask the classroom teacher whether they are aware of the Zones of Regulation or other similar programs and seek their permission to introduce the zones to the students you are working with.

Another strategy to help students identify their feelings and regulate their emotions is to check in with them throughout the day and ask how they are feeling or what emotions they are having. You can also read books with the students and talk about the feelings and emotions that characters have in the story. Older students can write in a journal or make up a story that explores their feelings. Helping students recognize their emotions is the first step toward their emotional self-regulation. With emotional recognition and regulation, prosocial skills get a huge lift, and being around others becomes much more enjoyable (Gray, 2015).

## Strategies for Teaching Social Skills

Many students who struggle with social-emotional health also struggle in their social relationships. While the development of social skills is a lifelong process, and not the sole responsibility of any one adult, you can play an important and supportive role in helping students build and strengthen these skills through everyday interactions and guided practice. Nancy Frey and colleagues (2022) highlight that the Illinois State Board of Education targets five social skills needed for success in life.

1. Recognize and manage emotions.
2. Demonstrate caring and concern for others.
3. Establish positive relationships.
4. Make responsible decisions.
5. Handle challenging situations constructively.

Students will develop and refine these skills throughout their lives, and many schools now offer formal instruction from a school counselor, teacher, or life-skills curriculum. However, you can greatly contribute to students' growth in these areas by modeling respectful communication, coaching students through peer conflicts, or facilitating structured practice. For example, role-playing real-life social situations or guiding students through a peer interaction can help students better interpret social cues, manage conflict, and build connections. Through these interactive sessions, students can better understand social cues, communication norms, and problem solving in various social situations. The goal is to equip students with the necessary skills for successful social interactions and foster positive relationships within the school community. Regular collaboration with teachers and other professionals will ensure that social skills training aligns with individual student needs and complements educational goals.

A growing number of online materials and books, such as *Social Emotional Stories: Lessons and Learning From Plants and Animals* (Lewis, 2021), provide high-interest stories with a focus on social skills for children of all ages. Students usually enjoy reading these social stories or having the stories read to them because they can relate to the featured characters and social issues. These stories typically end with a good resolution where the characters learn to handle themselves in a social situation or overcome a challenge. Using one of these stories, you can lead a robust discussion about the social skill and what happened in the narrative.

## Meet Mr. Carlson: Implementing Life-Skills Strategies

Leah, a tenth-grade student, has experienced significant trauma in her home life, which has contributed to ongoing emotional and behavioral challenges in the classroom. She frequently has emotional outbursts, quickly becomes angry when frustrated, and has broken down in tears on several occasions. Sarah often expresses a strong dislike for school and sometimes skips class or withdraws during group work.

Mr. Carlson, a paraprofessional, understands that supporting Leah's social-emotional health must take priority in order to help her succeed academically. He works closely with her and her teachers using a trauma-informed and relationship-centered approach, which includes the following strategies.

- **Trust and relationship building:** Mr. Carlson begins by establishing a supportive relationship with Leah, showing consistency, empathy, and genuine interest in her well-being. He avoids lecturing and instead listens actively during one-on-one conversations, which helps Leah feel seen and respected.

- **Understanding of emotional triggers:** Mr. Carlson collaborates with the school counselor to identify triggers that cause Leah distress, such as unexpected schedule changes, public criticism, and loud group dynamics. He discreetly shares this information with her teachers to ensure a more responsive classroom environment.

- **Predictable structure and academic support:** Knowing that predictability can help reduce anxiety, Mr. Carlson helps create a weekly planner and visual schedule for Leah's classes, including reminders for transitions, tests, and support sessions. This helps her feel more in control and better prepared.

- **Calm-down options:** In partnership with her teachers, Mr. Carlson ensures Leah has access to a designated quiet space on campus, such as a wellness room or counseling office, where she can go with permission when she's feeling overwhelmed. This space includes calming tools like noise-canceling headphones, stress balls, and journals.

- **Visual and digital supports:** Instead of elementary-style visual aids, Leah uses digital tools, such as a reminder app, a task tracker, and color-coded class folders, to stay organized and reduce executive function stress. Mr. Carlson helps her customize these tools to fit her preferences.

- **Emotional check-ins:** Mr. Carlson schedules informal check-ins with Leah throughout the week, sometimes just a quick chat before first period or a brief conversation during lunch. He uses these moments to gauge how she's doing emotionally and offer encouragement or space as needed.

- **Trauma-informed communication:** Mr. Carlson uses calm, nonjudgmental language and avoids power struggles. If Leah is escalated, he gives her time and space before reengaging and avoids phrases that she could perceive as dismissive or invalidating.

- **Coping skills and social-emotional growth:** Together, Mr. Carlson and Leah work on building her coping strategies, such as grounding techniques, breathing exercises, and journaling. He also encourages her to participate in a peer support group led by the school counselor, where she can practice relationship building and advocacy in a safe environment.

- **Flexibility and responsiveness:** Mr. Carlson recognizes that some days are harder than others for Leah. He stays flexible in his approach, adapting it based on how she shows up each day—sometimes offering academic scaffolding, other times simply providing space or connection.

Through this individualized, trauma-sensitive support system, Mr. Carlson helps Leah develop stronger self-regulation, build resilience, and reengage with learning. Within several weeks, she begins showing fewer outbursts and more consistent class attendance. She even starts contributing to group discussions and demonstrates renewed interest in her academic goals.

## Wrap-Up

This chapter shared information about working with students from a social-emotional or life-skills perspective. Now that you have considered common mental health challenges that students face and positive strategies for working with students on emotional regulation, relationship building, and problem solving, you are on your way to helping students learn critical skills that they will use for the rest of their lives. In the feature box that follows, you'll find practical advice from experienced paraprofessionals who work with students who need additional support in this area. Their insights are grounded in day-to-day experience. Then, in the "Notes and Reflections: Championing Social-Emotional Well-Being" reproducible (page 116), you'll have the opportunity to thoughtfully reflect on what you've learned and consider how these insights apply to your own practice.

## Advice From
### SUPERHERO PARAPROFESSIONALS

"Patience and empathy are key. Always try to see things from the student's perspective. Sometimes, a consistent, calm presence can make a difference."

(N. Simmons, personal communication, September 6, 2024)

"Building a trusting relationship takes time, but it's worth it. Once students know they can rely on you, they're more likely to open up and accept help."

(B. O'Brien, personal communication, November 8, 2024)

"Flexibility is important. What works for one student may not work for another. Be prepared to adapt your approach as needed."

(J. Griffin, personal communication, July 8, 2024)

# Notes and Reflections: Championing Social-Emotional Well-Being

Take a few moments to reflect on the following questions about being a superhero paraprofessional.

1. Reflect on a time in your personal life, a previous job, or your training when you observed a child or adolescent who showed signs of anxiety or depression. What did you notice? How did you respond, or how do you wish you had responded? If you haven't had this experience yet, consider how you might respond as a paraprofessional in the future. What signs would you look for, and what strategies would you try to support the student?

2. What strategies from this chapter do you feel most comfortable implementing? Why?

3. Consider a student you work with who may have experienced trauma. What steps can you take to create a more supportive environment for them?

4. How can you incorporate more social-emotional learning activities into your daily routine?

5. How can you best support a student who needs help with emotional regulation?

# 6

# Supporting Students With Learning Challenges

Every student deserves the opportunity to succeed, regardless of their learning differences. This is where we focus on inclusive education, ensuring that all students, including those with learning challenges, have the resources and support they need to thrive. The goal is to foster an environment where diverse learning needs are welcomed, acknowledged, and addressed. By doing so, we create classrooms that promote equity, engagement, and growth for every student.

Learning challenges can take many forms, from dyslexia and processing disorders to executive function difficulties. These challenges can impact a student's ability to read, write, focus, or retain information, and they often lead to frustration and a lack of confidence in their abilities. Without proper support, students with

## KEY POINTS

- Understand learning challenges.
- Create an inclusive environment.
- Use strategies to support students with learning challenges.
- Work with students who are English learners.
- Build self-advocacy skills and resilience in students.

learning challenges may struggle academically and socially, reinforcing a cycle of discouragement and disengagement. However, with the right strategies in place and the right superhero support, these students can develop the skills and resilience needed to succeed.

You play a critical role in leveling the playing field for students with learning challenges. By implementing research-based instructional strategies, fostering a positive and inclusive classroom culture, and collaborating with the classroom teacher and specialists, you can create a learning environment where all students feel valued and capable.

## Understanding Learning Challenges and How They Manifest

Every student learns differently, but for those with learning challenges, traditional teaching methods may not always be effective. Unlike the behavioral challenges discussed in chapter 4 or the social-emotional and mental health concerns explored in chapter 5, learning challenges are rooted in neurological processing differences that affect how students understand and use academic content. These difficulties are typically driven not by motivation, emotional regulation, or external behavior, but rather by how the brain processes language, numbers, sounds, visuals, or executive tasks. Learning challenges can affect how students process information, retain knowledge, and demonstrate understanding. By gaining a deeper understanding of these challenges, you can implement strategies that help students succeed.

Learning challenges can vary widely in how they affect students, but some of the most common include the following (Kemp, Smith, & Segal, 2025).

- **Dyslexia:** Dyslexia is a language-based learning disability that affects a student's ability to read accurately, fluently, and with comprehension. Students with dyslexia may struggle to recognize letters and their corresponding sounds, which impacts their phonemic awareness. Decoding words can be slow and laborious, making reading a challenging and often frustrating task. Spelling can also be difficult, as students may confuse letter sequences or omit letters altogether. Even when a student can sound out words, they may still struggle with reading comprehension. These challenges can significantly affect a student's confidence and academic performance, making targeted interventions and support essential.

- **Processing disorders:** Processing disorders impact the way the brain interprets auditory or visual input, creating difficulties in understanding spoken language, written text, or visual information. Auditory processing disorders can cause students to mishear instructions, struggle to distinguish sounds in noisy environments, or have difficulty following multistep directions. They may require instructions to be repeated or presented in written form to fully comprehend them. Visual processing disorders, on the other hand, can make it difficult for students to read maps, charts, or diagrams. Students might mix up similar-looking letters, such as *b* and *d*, or have trouble tracking words across a page, affecting their ability to read fluently and process visual information accurately.

- **Executive function challenges:** Executive function challenges affect a student's ability to effectively plan, organize, and complete tasks. These functions act as the brain's management system for navigating daily responsibilities. Students with executive function difficulties might forget to turn in assignments, even if they have completed them, due to struggles with organization. Time management can be another major hurdle, leading to procrastination or difficulty estimating how long a task will take. Following multistep directions can be overwhelming, and remembering important details can be challenging. Additionally, students with executive function challenges often struggle with transitions between activities or classes, making structured routines and support strategies essential.

- **Dysgraphia:** Dysgraphia is a writing-based learning disability that affects a student's ability to write legibly and express their thoughts on paper. Students with dysgraphia may have poor handwriting that is difficult to read, trouble forming letters correctly or spacing words properly, and difficulty organizing their thoughts in written form. Even if they can express their ideas verbally, translating them into written sentences can be a significant challenge. Accommodations such as speech-to-text technology, graphic organizers, and alternative writing methods can help these students succeed.

- **Dyscalculia:** Dyscalculia is a mathematics-based learning disability that affects a student's ability to understand numbers and mathematics concepts. Students with dyscalculia may struggle with basic number sense, such as understanding that the numeral 5 represents five objects. Memorizing mathematics facts, such as multiplication tables, can be particularly difficult, as can solving multistep mathematics problems or recognizing numerical patterns. Because mathematics concepts build on one another, early intervention and the use of visual aids, manipulatives, and step-by-step problem-solving strategies can help students with dyscalculia develop stronger mathematics skills.

Learning challenges can manifest in the classroom in a variety of ways that make it difficult for students to fully engage with the curriculum. While some struggles are more noticeable, others may be subtle and mistaken for a lack of effort or motivation. Recognizing these signs early can help educators provide the right support and interventions.

- **Academic struggles:** These struggles are some of the most apparent indicators of a learning challenge. Students may have persistent difficulties with reading fluency, comprehension, writing, or mathematics problems, even when they are putting in effort and receiving instruction. They might avoid reading aloud, struggle with spelling, or have difficulty organizing their thoughts in written assignments. In mathematics, they may find it hard to grasp numerical concepts, memorize facts, or follow multistep problem-solving processes.

- **Attention and focus issues:** Attention issues can make it challenging for students to stay on task, follow through with assignments, or absorb new information. These students may seem easily distracted by their surroundings, frequently look away from their work, or have difficulty sustaining attention during lessons. They might also start assignments but struggle to complete them or require frequent redirection from teachers and support staff.

- **Slow processing speed:** Slower processing means that a student may take longer than their peers to read instructions, grasp new concepts, or respond to questions. They might struggle to keep up with classroom discussions, complete timed tests, or quickly process verbal information. This can lead to frustration, as they may understand the material but need extra time to demonstrate their knowledge.

- **Memory difficulties:** Memory challenges can impact both short-term and long-term recall, making it hard for students to remember instructions, retain new vocabulary, or apply previously learned skills. They may frequently forget what they were supposed to do after receiving directions, misplace materials like their homework or notebooks, or need repeated exposure to concepts before they stick.

- **Language processing disorders:** Language challenges can make it difficult for students to effectively understand and use spoken language. Students with receptive language disorders may struggle with following multistep directions, misunderstand questions, or require additional time to process verbal information. Those with expressive language difficulties may have trouble finding the right words, forming coherent sentences, or clearly expressing their thoughts. These challenges can affect both academic performance and social interactions.

- **Emotional and behavioral responses:** Emotional and behavioral challenges often accompany learning difficulties, as students may feel overwhelmed, frustrated, or anxious when faced with academic tasks they find challenging. Some students may withdraw from or avoid tasks that seem too difficult, while others may act out by becoming disruptive or defiant. They might express feelings of inadequacy, struggle with low self-esteem, or exhibit anxiety-related behaviors, such as frequent stomachaches or reluctance to participate in class.

Learning about these signs will help you realize that students are not trying to behave badly but instead are asking for help to get their learning and social needs met. As a superhero paraprofessional, you can be there for these students and make a huge difference.

Despite growing awareness, several misconceptions about learning challenges persist. These myths can contribute to misunderstandings and create barriers to student success. The more aware you are of these myths, the more you can help dispel them.

- **Myth:** Students with learning challenges are not intelligent.
  - *Reality*—Learning challenges have nothing to do with intelligence. Many students with dyslexia, dyscalculia, or other difficulties are highly creative, analytic, or skilled in nontraditional ways (Girard-Joyal & Gauthier, 2021).
- **Myth:** The students just need to try harder.
  - *Reality*—Learning challenges are not a matter of effort. Students with these difficulties often work twice as hard as their peers to keep up. They need effective strategies and accommodations, not just increased effort (Shaywitz & Shaywitz, 2020).
- **Myth:** Accommodations give some students unfair advantages.
  - *Reality*—Accommodations level the playing field by providing students with the tools they need to demonstrate their abilities. They do not make tasks easier but rather make learning accessible (Blasey, Wang, & Blasey, 2022).

- **Myth:** Learning challenges can be outgrown.
  - *Reality*—While students can develop strategies to manage their difficulties, learning challenges often persist into adulthood. With the right support, students can learn to work around their challenges and achieve success (Fletcher, Lyon, Fuchs, & Barnes, 2019).

By understanding the realities of learning challenges, you can take part in creating an environment that fosters patience, inclusion, and success for all students. You can meet students where they are and celebrate all their strengths and wins while helping them in the areas that are challenging.

## Creating an Inclusive Learning Environment

Creating an inclusive learning environment means ensuring that every student has the opportunity to succeed, regardless of their abilities, background, or challenges.

> You can meet students where they are and celebrate all their strengths and wins while helping them in the areas that are challenging.

This involves adopting strategies and practices that meet the diverse needs of learners. Well-used methods include Universal Design for Learning and differentiated instruction strategies.

### Universal Design for Learning Principles

Universal Design for Learning is a framework that provides flexibility in how content is delivered, how students engage with the material, and how they demonstrate their learning. The core ideas are to create a learning environment that is accessible to all students, removes barriers to learning, and offers multiple pathways for success, such as the following (Stapleton-Corcoran, 2022).

- **Multiple means of engagement:** Universal Design for Learning encourages teachers to engage students through various methods that tap into their interests, motivations, and learning preferences. They could offer choices in how students engage with lessons, such as through collaborative projects, hands-on activities, or independent research. In your work, you might assist students in exploring different activities or provide additional support to ensure that all students are participating actively, meaningfully, and in a manner that is linked to their interests.

- **Multiple means of representation:** Students process information in different ways, and Universal Design for Learning encourages teachers' use of multiple formats to present material. These formats might include visual aids, interactive activities, oral presentations, or multimedia resources. You play a critical role here by helping students access these materials in ways that best suit their individual needs. For example, you may read text aloud for students who struggle with reading comprehension or provide additional clarification on complex concepts.

- **Multiple means of expression:** Universal Design for Learning recognizes that students express their learning in different ways. While some students may excel at written tasks, others may prefer oral presentations, creative projects, or digital media. By offering encouragement, guidance, and alternative methods of expression when necessary, you can support students in their learning and provide them with a positive learning experience where they show you what they know and are able to do.

Universal Design for Learning can help you ensure that all students have access to the resources and support needed to engage, learn, and express themselves in the classroom.

### Differentiated Instruction Strategies

Differentiated instruction and Universal Design for Learning go hand in hand. Differentiation is an instructional approach that tailors teaching methods to meet the diverse needs of students. By recognizing that each student learns in unique ways, differentiated instruction allows educators to provide a variety of learning experiences and supports, and to improve academics and behavior as a result (Sisson, 2022).

Differentiated instruction requires providing multiple means of representation; you present information in various formats to accommodate different learning preferences. Differentiation also involves offering multiple ways for students to express their understanding, such as project-based learning, collaborative discussions, visual or digital presentations, or technology-enhanced responses. For example, you may use graphic organizers, audiobooks, and hands-on activities to engage students and enhance their understanding of literacy concepts. You can also offer students multiple choices or opportunities to engage in literacy instruction and meaningfully demonstrate their understanding. You can incorporate project-based learning, collaborative activities, and technology tools to motivate students and foster their interest in literacy.

It's important to note that differentiation doesn't require *every* assignment to be tailored to each student's preferred learning style. Instead, the goal is to design instruction across a unit that includes a variety of learning formats. This ensures that all students will at times learn in a way that suits them, while also being encouraged to stretch and engage in less familiar or comfortable formats—an important part of developing adaptable learners.

As a superhero paraprofessional, you can implement these strategies by working closely with students in small groups or individually, providing targeted and differentiated support as needed. Here are some ways that you can use differentiation in the classroom (Sisson, 2022).

- **Content differentiation:** Differentiating content means adjusting the material to meet students' readiness levels and interests. This could involve offering varied reading materials, tasks of different complexity levels, or visual aids to support comprehension. You may provide additional resources or simplify materials to ensure all students can access the content at their own level.

- **Process differentiation:** Differentiating the process involves offering various ways for students to engage with the content. For example, a lesson might include small-group discussions, peer collaboration, and individual practice. As a paraprofessional, you can facilitate these activities, offer explanations, and assist students who need additional guidance to stay on track.

- **Product differentiation:** Differentiated instruction allows students to demonstrate their learning in different ways, whether through written reports, oral presentations, or creative projects. You can provide the scaffolding necessary for students to complete these tasks. For example, you might assist students with organizing thoughts for a written assignment or structuring a presentation.

By supporting differentiated instruction, you can ensure that your students have access to the lesson and are also appropriately challenged to stay engaged and keep growing.

## Implementing Effective Strategies for Supporting Students

Supporting students in an inclusive classroom involves providing tailored strategies that meet the unique needs of each learner. Effective support is not just about helping students understand the material—it's about creating an environment where they feel confident, capable, and engaged in their learning. Research has shown that differentiated, multisensory, and inclusive teaching practices contribute to improved academic outcomes, engagement, and self-efficacy for students with varied learning needs (Brock, 2021; CAST, 2024).

### Multisensory Learning Strategies

Multisensory learning engages more than one sense at a time, creating more opportunities for students to connect with the material. This approach is particularly effective for students with learning disabilities, English learners, and those who need additional support in processing information (Birsh & Carreker, 2018). Multisensory strategies can include a combination of visual, auditory, kinesthetic, and tactile learning experiences. For example, suppose you are working with a student who struggles in mathematics. In that case, you can use mathematics games and interactive activities to make practice engaging and enjoyable and help the student develop a positive attitude toward mathematics. Many students who struggle in mathematics have a negative attitude toward the subject, so making mathematics fun and helping them experience success are important.

Here's how you can present information to students in ways that incorporate different senses.

- **Visual learning:** Using images, videos, charts, and diagrams can reinforce concepts for visual learners. Many students thrive with visual supports, and you can ensure they have access to these visual tools and assist them in interpreting the tools or creating their own visual representations of the material. Research shows that visual representations support comprehension and retention, especially for students with learning disabilities and English learners (CAST, 2024; Marzano, 2005).

- **Auditory learning:** Incorporating music, spoken word, and sound cues into lessons can support auditory learners. Verbal repetition, read-alouds, and oral discussion promote processing and comprehension for many students, including those with auditory learning strengths or processing challenges (Vaughn & Bos, 2015). You might assist by reading instructions aloud, reinforcing verbal directions, or helping students record their responses orally.

- **Kinesthetic learning:** Many students learn best through movement or hands-on activities. You can support kinesthetic learners by facilitating interactive tasks such as building models, conducting experiments, or using physical manipulatives to illustrate concepts. Encouraging students to use their hands and bodies to engage with learning can make abstract ideas more tangible. Kinesthetic learning strategies are linked to increased engagement and improved academic performance, particularly when students can physically manipulate materials to understand abstract concepts (Brock, 2021; Tomlinson, 2014).

- **Tactile learning:** Tactile learning involves touch-based materials that enhance sensory engagement. Tactile strategies support memory formation and engagement, especially in early learners or students with sensory integration needs (Birsh & Carreker, 2018). For example, tools like textured flash cards or letter tiles can reinforce letter recognition, spelling, and mathematics concepts.

You are key to presenting information in different ways and providing hands-on support so that students actively engage with lessons in ways that suit their individual needs.

### Tasks Broken Down Into Manageable Steps

Breaking down complex tasks into smaller, more manageable steps is one of the most effective ways to support students, especially those who may struggle with organization, focus, or task completion. This approach not only helps students feel less overwhelmed but also provides a clear pathway to success. Breaking down a task into manageable steps involves the following.

- **Chunking of information:** Rather than giving students long, complex instructions, break the task into smaller segments or "chunks." You can guide students through each chunk, ensuring they understand the task before moving on to the next step. This approach maintains students' focus and reduces the cognitive load required to complete the assignment.

- **Clear instructions:** Clear, simple instructions help students understand what is expected of them. You can clarify directions, check for student understanding, and offer examples or nonexamples to demonstrate the task. You may also provide additional reminders or visual cues to help students stay on track throughout the task.

- **Frequent check-ins:** You play a crucial role in monitoring students' progress and providing timely feedback. You can check in frequently to ensure students are making progress, redirect them if necessary, and offer support if a student encounters a challenge. This ongoing guidance prevents students from feeling stuck and ensures they can complete tasks with confidence.

- **Celebrations of small wins:** Breaking tasks into smaller steps allows students to experience success along the way. You can provide praise and reinforcement when students complete individual steps to foster a sense of accomplishment and motivation to continue working.

By breaking tasks into manageable chunks, you can limit students' anxiety and give them the structure they need to tackle challenging assignments successfully.

### Effective Instructional Strategies

Effective instructional strategies go beyond traditional teaching methods; they incorporate diverse approaches that support students' varied learning preferences and abilities. Some of these strategies include active learning, instruction scaffolded with the gradual release of responsibility method, and recasting and reteaching. You are essential in providing the necessary assistance to implement these strategies and create an environment where students feel more engaged and capable of succeeding.

#### Active Learning

Encouraging students to actively participate in their learning deepens their understanding and retention. Active learning can involve activities such as discussions, hands-on projects, role plays, or interactive group work. You can facilitate small-group activities or provide one-on-one support during whole-class discussions, ensuring that students who need extra attention are included and able to participate fully.

#### Scaffolded Instruction

Scaffolding involves providing temporary support to students until they can independently complete a task. You can assist by breaking down tasks, offering hints, or providing additional practice opportunities. As students master the skills, you gradually reduce your support. You may also reinforce key concepts and check on students to ensure they are progressing toward independence.

A commonly used scaffolding technique is gradual release of responsibility (Fisher & Frey, 2021). In this structured method, instructors gradually shift the responsibility of learning from themselves to the student to empower the student to become more independent. This process begins with "I do it," where you model the task, providing clear and explicit instructions. After you model, move to guided practice with the student ("We do it"). In this stage, you can offer prompts, ask guiding questions, and provide encouragement. Next, move into peer collaboration ("You do it together"). This collaborative learning environment allows students to learn from each other, share strategies, and offer mutual support. In the final stage, you gradually step back as students independently apply the skill ("You do it alone"). At this stage, you become an observer and occasional facilitator, stepping in only if necessary.

Celebrating students' successes and providing positive reinforcement to build their self-efficacy and motivation are essential. Throughout the lesson, remember to use check-ins, visual aids, and feedback to ensure students feel supported while they're gaining ownership of their learning.

### Recasting and Reteaching Strategies

The classroom teacher often provides you with a lesson plan and activities to do with a student or group of students. Follow the lesson plan and ask for clarification if you need it. The lesson plan is a road map the teacher has designed to effectively guide instructional time and ensure that learning objectives are met. By following the lesson plan, you help maintain consistency and structure in the classroom, which are essential for student learning. However, some students must be taught certain material several times and in different ways to grasp and remember it. This is where superhero paraprofessionals come in to reteach and recast the material. Recognizing when students are struggling and knowing how to adapt the lesson through recasting and reteaching can significantly impact their understanding and retention.

Recasting involves rephrasing information or presenting it differently when a student does not understand the initial explanation. This technique is beneficial in real time during lessons. For instance, if a student seems confused by a mathematics concept, you might use more straightforward language, visual aids, or concrete examples to explain it again. Recasting helps clarify misunderstandings and provides students with multiple ways to comprehend the material. As a paraprofessional, you can be attentive to students' cues and ready to step in with alternative explanations while ensuring you reinforce the teacher's instructional goals and don't deviate from the lesson plan.

Reteaching is a more intensive strategy that you use when a significant portion of the class or an individual student has yet to grasp a concept despite initial instruction. This might occur during a dedicated review session or immediately after an assessment reveals gaps in understanding. Reteaching involves reviewing the material using different methods and additional practice opportunities. For instance, if students struggle with a reading comprehension passage, you might break down the text into smaller sections, use graphic organizers to map out key ideas, and engage students in discussions to deepen their understanding. Reteaching requires patience and creativity, as it often involves finding new ways to present the same content to make it more accessible.

### Visual Aids, Graphic Organizers, and Color Coding

Visual aids, graphic organizers, and color coding are powerful tools for helping all students process and retain information, especially students learning English. These tools can simplify complex ideas, make abstract concepts more concrete, and provide students with visual representations of their learning.

- **Visual aids:** Items such as charts, diagrams, pictures, and videos can illustrate key concepts. You can ensure that these aids are readily available to students and assist with interpreting or creating them. You might also help students connect the visuals to their learning, reinforcing how the visuals support their understanding of the content.

- **Graphic organizers:** Graphic organizers, such as Venn diagrams, concept maps, and storyboards, help students organize and synthesize information. You can work with students to complete graphic organizers, providing guidance on how to categorize information, identify key points, or create visual representations of their thoughts.

- **Color coding:** Color-coded information can make learning more accessible by differentiating key concepts or ideas for students. You and the classroom teacher can decide on color-coded materials, and you can guide students in using color to make connections between concepts.

## Supporting Multilingual Learners in the Classroom

Supporting English learners (also known as *multilingual learners*) in the classroom is an important role you may find yourself filling. These students often face the challenge of learning academic content while simultaneously acquiring a new language. It's essential to understand that limited English proficiency is not a reflection of a student's intelligence, capability, or depth of understanding. Too often, educators unintentionally underestimate students' abilities due to language barriers, which can result in students being denied access to grade-level instruction they are fully capable of understanding and engaging with, especially once given the proper support.

As a paraprofessional, you can play a vital part in helping multilingual learners succeed both academically and socially. An effective way to support these students is by providing language scaffolds that make content accessible. A key concept in supporting language development is *comprehensible input*, which means presenting content in ways that students can understand while continuing to develop language proficiency. This can include using visuals, realia (real-life objects), gestures, simplified but not watered-down language, and clear modeling. Small-group or one-on-one support is also highly effective in reinforcing academic vocabulary and clarifying concepts (Echevarría, Vogt, & Short, 2017).

### Using Assistive Technology to Support Inclusive Learning

Supporting multilingual learners also means ensuring they have equitable access to tools that support their language development and learning, especially when those tools overlap with supports used by students with diverse learning needs. Rather than isolating assistive technology as a separate resource, you should understand it as part of a broader inclusive learning environment.

Assistive technology provides students with multiple means to access, process, and demonstrate their understanding in ways that align with their unique abilities. You play an important role in ensuring that these tools are used effectively, make learning more accessible, and help students stay engaged.

- **Speech-to-text software:** This tool allows students who struggle with writing to express ideas verbally. You can assist students in setting up and using these tools and provide guidance on how to dictate their responses and correct any errors that may arise. You can also help students practice using speech-to-text technology in different contexts, whether they are working on writing assignments, taking notes, or completing exams. This tool benefits multilingual learners by reducing the cognitive load of writing in a new language.

- **Audiobooks and text-to-speech tools:** These tools support students with reading difficulties or visual impairments. Audiobooks and text-to-speech tools are essential for students with dyslexia, students with visual impairments, or students learning another language. You can ensure that students have access to these tools and help them set up and navigate these resources.

- **Learning management systems and digital tools:** Digital platforms can help students stay organized and easily access materials. You can assist students in using these systems to stay organized and manage their tasks more efficiently. You may help students set reminders, monitor their progress, and effectively use online resources.

In addition to software tools, there are a variety of adaptive tools that support reading, writing, and organization.

- **Graphic organizers:** Graphic organizers are valuable tools for students who struggle with organizing information because they help students break down complex tasks and synthesize information visually. You can assist students in using these tools, whether digitally or on paper, to organize their thoughts and structure their writing.

- **Reading supports:** Tools such as highlighter pens, overlays, or digital apps that adjust text size and color contrast can help students with visual impairments or attention difficulties engage with reading materials. You can ensure that these tools are available and help students learn how to use them effectively.

- **Organizational tools:** For students who have difficulty with organization, adaptive tools such as planners, binders with labeled dividers, and digital calendars can help them manage their tasks. You can work with students to set up and maintain these systems, offering support when students need it to prioritize tasks or keep track of deadlines.

### Teaching Vocabulary in Three Tiers

As a paraprofessional, you can help students learn English by developing their academic language skills. This may involve teaching vocabulary, grammar, and language structures specific to the content area. You can also provide opportunities for students to practice speaking, listening, reading, and writing in English. The more practice they get using their English skills in a safe environment, the better their English skills will become (Katz, 2025).

An integral part of teaching language skills is increasing students' vocabulary. Teaching vocabulary is important for all students, but it's especially important for students learning English. To ensure students understand and use new words in various contexts involves a multitiered approach (McKeown, 2019). Here's an explanation of the tiers of vocabulary instruction and types of words.

- **Tier 1 (basic vocabulary):** Tier 1 words are common words that students are likely to frequently encounter and already know, such as *dog, happy,* and *run.* These words often refer to familiar objects, actions, or concepts. To teach these words, make sure that students use them accurately in different contexts, and have students practice and repeat them often to really learn them.

- **Tier 2 (high-frequency and academic vocabulary):** More complex and less common than Tier 1 words, these words are not used as frequently in everyday conversation but are found in academic texts and more formal writing. Examples include *analyze, concept,* and *contrast.* These words are essential for academic success in many different subjects. Teach these words directly by defining them and giving examples and nonexamples. Encourage your students to use the words often to become more comfortable with them.

- **Tier 3 (domain-specific vocabulary):** Tier 3 words are specific to particular fields or subjects, such as *photosynthesis* in science and *monarch* in history. They are not frequently used outside their specific academic or professional contexts. To help students learn them, provide clear explanations and definitions related to the subject matter. Use diagrams, visuals, and real-world examples to aid understanding. Encourage students to use these terms in the context of their study subject and in projects, presentations, or discussions (McKeown, 2019).

### Teaching Vocabulary for All Tiers

Teaching vocabulary effectively involves more than just memorization; it requires engaging students in ways that help them internalize and apply new words. Here are several techniques that can enhance vocabulary instruction.

- **Preteaching of vocabulary:** Introducing key vocabulary in advance helps students build background knowledge, which improves their comprehension and confidence. You can preteach vocabulary through discussions, visuals, or simple definitions to give students a foundation for understanding.

- **Contextual learning:** Learning vocabulary in context—through reading passages, classroom discussions, and writing exercises—allows students to see how words function in real language. For example, instead of simply defining the word *resilient,* students might read a short story about a character who overcomes challenges and discuss how the word applies to the situation.

- **Interactive activities:** Make vocabulary learning engaging and fun. Games like charades, word sorts, and crossword puzzles reinforce word meanings in playful ways. You can have students use flash cards to match words to definitions or pictures, and interactive technology, such as vocabulary apps, can provide additional reinforcement. Encouraging students to see vocabulary learning as enjoyable can boost their motivation.

- **Frequent review:** Repetition through varied activities—such as word walls, vocabulary journals, and collaborative review games—reinforces and deepens students' understanding. The more exposure students have to a word in different contexts, the more likely they are to remember it and use it accurately.

- **Encouragement of use:** Give students regular opportunities to use new words in journal entries, essays, group discussions, and presentations. Sentence starters or open-ended questions can prompt students to naturally incorporate new vocabulary into their language use. The more they practice, the more comfortable and confident they will become in applying their expanding vocabulary.

You can help students build a strong vocabulary that supports their academic and everyday language needs by teaching all vocabulary tiers (McKeown, 2019). Work with your classroom teacher to identify key terms students need to know, and then jump in and start teaching them.

In addition to providing language support, you must help create a culturally responsive classroom environment. Culturally responsive teaching honors the identities, values, and experiences of all students. You can help by learning about your students' backgrounds, encouraging your students to share their cultural perspectives, and ensuring classroom visuals, stories, and activities reflect diverse cultures and languages. This not only makes students feel seen and valued but also enriches the classroom experience for all students.

## Building Self-Advocacy Skills and Resilience in Students

Self-advocacy is the ability to express one's needs and take responsibility for one's own learning and well-being. Developing self-advocacy is particularly important for students with learning challenges, as it empowers them to seek support when needed and make decisions about their education. Resilience is the ability to recover from setbacks and persist in the face of challenges. Here are some ways you can help promote self-advocacy and resilience.

- **Modeling self-advocacy:** You can model self-advocacy behaviors by demonstrating how to ask for help, express feelings, and articulate learning needs. By observing how you self-advocate, students learn how to communicate their needs effectively in the classroom and beyond.

- **Encouraging reflection:** You can have students reflect on their learning experiences and behavior. Asking guiding questions like "What worked well for you today?" or "What could help you succeed next time?" encourages students to think critically about their actions and recognize the importance of advocating for their own success.

- **Facilitating goal setting:** Helping students set personal goals is another way you can encourage self-advocacy. By setting small, attainable goals and helping students track their progress, you teach students to take ownership of their learning and their emotional development. Celebrating these successes builds students' confidence in their ability to advocate for themselves.

- **Promoting effort over perfection:** A growth mindset focuses on effort, improvement, and the learning process rather than perfection. You can maintain this focus by praising students for their persistence, creativity, and problem-solving skills. By celebrating the journey rather than just the outcome, you can contribute to building a classroom culture where all students feel valued for their efforts.

- **Fostering resilience:** You can help students develop this skill by supporting them when they encounter difficulties. Whether through emotional encouragement, additional practice, or problem-solving strategies, you can help students navigate challenges and learn how to bounce back stronger. For students who struggle with frustration, having you near can be the reassurance they need to keep going.

- **Encouraging risk taking:** Students with a growth mindset are more likely to take risks and try new things, knowing that mistakes are part of the learning process. You can support this by creating a safe and supportive environment where students feel comfortable taking risks. Whether you're offering a gentle nudge to try a new activity or helping students reflect on their mistakes in a positive light, you can foster an atmosphere where resilience flourishes.

By promoting self-advocacy and resilience, you can empower students to tackle challenges, persist through difficulties, and take pride in their progress, regardless of how big or small it is.

## Monitoring Progress

Effective teaching involves continuously checking on students' progress and understanding throughout the lesson. You play a key role by monitoring students' responses and providing feedback. You can also support students who need further clarification or individualized assistance, ensuring that no student is left behind.

There are many ways to check for understanding or assess a student's progress. A wide range of assessments can monitor learning, so you and your classroom teacher will need to discuss and decide on the assessment you will use and how you will collect the data. Table 6.1 provides an overview of the most commonly used types of assessments and ways to monitor students' progress.

**Table 6.1: Assessments of Student Learning and Progress**

| Assessment Type | Assessment Description |
|---|---|
| Running Records | A running record is a formative assessment tool used to observe and record a student's reading behavior as they read aloud. It helps identify the student's reading level, accuracy, and comprehension skills. |
| Anecdotal Notes | Anecdotal notes are informal narrative records of observations made by teachers about students' behaviors, skills, and academic performance. These notes provide insights into student progress over time. |
| Student Observations | These systematic observations during classroom activities are used to gather information about students' learning processes, interactions, and behaviors. The observations can be structured or unstructured. |
| Exit Tickets | These brief assessments are given at the end of a lesson or class to gauge students' understanding of the material that was taught. Students write responses to questions or summarize critical points learned. |
| Exams and Quizzes | These formal assessments evaluate student learning and understanding of specific content. They can include multiple-choice questions, short-answer questions, essay questions, and other question formats to measure knowledge and skills. |
| Performance Assessment | On a performance assessment, students demonstrate their knowledge and skills by performing a task or creating a product. This type of assessment focuses on applying learning in real-world or practical contexts. |

## Using Ongoing Assessment in the Paraprofessional's Role

The overall goal of ongoing assessment is to understand where students are in their learning so that instruction can be tailored to their specific needs. There is no single best way to assess, yet using a wide variety of assessment methods provides a more complete picture of each student's progress and challenges. As a paraprofessional, you may not be responsible for designing or grading formal assessments, but you play an important supporting role in the assessment process.

You work closely with the teacher to observe students during instruction and activities, take notes on student performance and behavior, and provide feedback about how students are responding to different strategies or content. You might assist with administering informal assessments, such as running records, checklists, or comprehension questions, or gathering student work samples. Your observations and insights can help the teacher make informed decisions about how to adjust instruction, group students, or provide additional support. Regular communication and collaboration with the teacher ensure that assessment is a shared, ongoing process that directly informs teaching and learning.

## Meet Maria: Supporting English Learners

Maria has been a paraprofessional at Lincoln High School for three years. With a background in bilingual education and a deep understanding of cultural diversity, she is well equipped to support English learners. Maria's primary role involves working with students from various cultural backgrounds, helping them improve their English proficiency, and ensuring they feel included and respected within the school community. Here is how she accomplishes that.

- **Preparing and following a morning routine:** Maria begins her day by reviewing the lesson plans prepared by the lead teacher, Mr. Nichols. She pays special attention to sections that might pose challenges for EL students. Maria prepares visual aids, bilingual dictionaries, and culturally relevant examples to help bridge language gaps.

- **Working with students:** One of Maria's key responsibilities is to provide one-on-one or small-group instruction to EL students. In first period, she works with five ninth-grade students at different levels of English language acquisition. Maria starts the session with a warm-up activity that involves sharing words from their native languages and translating them into English, which builds their vocabulary and values their linguistic backgrounds.

- **Recasting and reteaching:** During a mathematics lesson, for example, Maria notices that a student named Ahmed needs help understanding the concept of ratios. She uses recasting to explain the idea in more straightforward English and relate it to a real-life context that Ahmed is familiar with. When Ahmed continues to struggle, Maria schedules a reteaching session. She uses visual aids like multiplication charts and hands-on activities involving objects to make the concept more tangible. This approach helps Ahmed grasp the concept more effectively.

- **Being culturally sensitive and inclusive:** Maria is acutely aware of the cultural nuances that can impact learning. For example, she understands that some students might come from educational backgrounds where speaking up in class is discouraged. To address this, Maria creates a safe and supportive environment by using positive reinforcement and encouraging participation through pair and group work, where students might feel more comfortable speaking. Maria also incorporates students' cultural backgrounds into the curriculum.

- **Reflecting and continuously improving:** At the end of each week, Maria reflects on the effectiveness of her strategies by discussing them with Mr. Nichols and the EL coordinator. They review student progress and adjust their approaches as needed. Maria also attends workshops on cultural competency and language acquisition to continue improving her skills.

Maria's success as a paraprofessional lies in her ability to combine educational support with cultural sensitivity. By using recasting and reteaching strategies, working hard to foster an inclusive classroom environment, and maintaining strong communication with the classroom teacher, she helps her students improve their English proficiency and feel valued and respected.

## Wrap-Up

This chapter provided valuable insights into working with students who face a variety of learning challenges. It explored some of the most common challenges and offered practical strategies for effectively supporting these students. For students learning English, the chapter also introduced instructional approaches tailored to their unique needs. In the feature box that follows, you'll find practical advice from experienced paraprofessionals who support students requiring additional assistance. Their insights are grounded in day-to-day experience. Then, in the "Notes and Reflections: Supporting Students With Learning Challenges" reproducible (page 138), you'll have the opportunity to thoughtfully reflect on what you've learned and consider how these insights apply to your own practice.

## *Advice From*
### SUPERHERO PARAPROFESSIONALS

"Incorporate students' cultural backgrounds into lessons. Be interested in their story. This makes learning more relatable and meaningful for them."

(M. Lopez, personal communication, November 1, 2024)

"Encourage students to share their languages and cultures with their peers. Encourage them to be proud of what makes them who they are."

(M. Jones, personal communication, October 23, 2024)

"Always meet students where they are. The English language is hard to learn! Use their strengths to help them overcome their challenges. Remember, patience and persistence are your greatest tools."

(M. Patterson, personal communication, September 1, 2024)

# Notes and Reflections: Supporting Students With Learning Challenges

Take a few moments to reflect on the following questions about being a superhero paraprofessional.

1. In your role, how can you incorporate differentiated instruction strategies to better support students with diverse learning needs?

2. What informal assessment methods can you use to effectively track students' academic progress?

3. How can you help students strengthen their resilience in the classroom?

4. What new technologies can you explore to assist teachers with technology integration in the classroom?

5. What strategies would you feel comfortable using with a student who has learning challenges?

# 7

# Serving as the Main Educator

M ost states require a lead teacher to have the necessary credentials in order to serve in that role. Yet sometimes, things happen that cause a paraprofessional to have to step in as the primary teacher.

- A teacher falls ill during the day and needs to leave suddenly but no one else is available.

- A teacher needs to take an extended leave, and the school cannot find a credentialed substitute teacher to take the class.

- A substitute is found but needs help with the routines and schedules and heavily relies on the paraprofessional to keep things as normal as possible.

- The paraprofessional has a teaching credential while serving as a paraprofessional, and the school asks them to change hats and step in as the substitute teacher.

## KEY POINTS

- Prepare to be the primary educator.

- Make successful lesson plans.

- Create AI-generated lesson plans.

- Learn interactive instructional strategies that can keep student engagement high.

Whatever the reason, you might be called on as the primary educator, and therefore, you need to be prepared with a solid knowledge base and the adaptability to take on the teacher's responsibilities during their absence. It is essential that you work closely with the regular teacher, if possible, to ensure continuity in curriculum and teaching methods.

Serving as the primary instructor is a real superhero move that requires additional skills and preparation. You must be prepared to lead all aspects of the lesson, from introducing new concepts to facilitating discussions and monitoring student progress. While stepping into this lead teaching role can be daunting, it also presents an opportunity for you to showcase your capabilities and grow professionally. With the right mindset, you can rise to the occasion and provide a positive learning experience for students in the teacher's absence.

As a paraprofessional stepping into the role of the primary educator, you must understand the full extent of your responsibilities, which include managing the classroom and maintaining order and structure at all times. You also need to be able to deliver lessons and provide clear explanations to students while helping them complete assignments to ensure learning continues without interruption. Inevitably, some students will need individual support from you, and you will soon identify who those students are and provide them with that extra support.

When asked to take over the teaching responsibilities in a classroom, you also need to communicate effectively with the school administration and office manager. Keep them informed of the classroom's progress and any challenges you encounter. Regular updates will help them understand your situation and provide necessary support. Seek out colleagues, as they can also be significant sources of support. Reach out to experienced paraprofessionals or teachers for advice and mentorship. Their insights can help you better adapt to your new role. Sharing resources, strategies, and experiences can foster a collaborative environment that benefits you and your students. You've got this!

## Practical Strategies for Success

When stepping into the role of the primary teacher in the room, even for a short period of time, you can follow these foundational practices to create a structured routine for the students and yourself.

- **Daily schedule:** Start by creating a schedule for each day you will be with the class. If you don't know how long you will be there, make your plans two days at a time. This way, if the teacher returns, they will have a daily schedule ready. For consistency, keep the same daily schedule that the students are used to if at all possible. Write the schedule on the board for all to see; it can help you stay on track throughout the day.

- **Classroom routines:** Stick to established routines to help students feel secure and know what to expect. Remind the students of the routines and explain that things will run the same way they always do even though the classroom teacher is absent. For example, make sure that students sit where they are supposed to sit, remind them of the classroom rules and the consequences for not following those rules, and use the classroom's established procedures. Ask helpful students about these routines if they are unclear to you.

- **Clear expectations:** Communicate your expectations for behavior and classroom conduct from the start. You are in charge and need to sound and act in charge. Remind students of the classroom rules and behavioral expectations, the positive rewards they can earn, and the consequences they might face for not following the rules.

Access the teacher's lesson plans if possible. If they are unavailable, use your knowledge of the curriculum to create a simple, structured plan for each day. Most states and provinces have their own standards (as might your district), which you can find online and use to determine the topics to teach at your grade level. There is no one right way to plan a lesson, but the following sections offer suggestions for designing lesson plans, applying AI to the lesson design process, and creating interactive lessons that foster student engagement.

### Lesson Plan Design

Designing your lesson plan so that it is clear and manageable for the teacher and students involves the following key components.

- **Objective: Know what you are trying to teach**—Clearly define what students should know or be able to do by the end of the lesson. What are you going to teach them? Clarity helps all lessons go better.

- **Standards: Know the standards your lesson aligns with**—Ensure that the lesson relates to relevant educational standards and meets required educational guidelines. Most states and provinces have standards for subjects and grade levels that you should consult.

- **Materials and resources: Have the right items ready**—Determine all the materials and resources you need for your lesson, including textbooks, handouts, technology, and other supplies. Ensure that you have everything ready before the lesson begins.

- **Differentiation: Plan for different learners**—Plan for diverse learners by incorporating strategies to address varied needs, learning preferences, and abilities. This might include modifying tasks, providing additional resources, or offering alternative assignments for students who need more support or challenge. Planning before the lesson can reduce behavioral or emotional issues that arise from frustrated students who need additional help or find the lesson too easy.

- **Introduction: Get students hooked**—Start with an engaging activity or question that captures students' interest and introduces the lesson topic. This can be a story, a question, a video clip, or an interesting fact related to the lesson.

- **Direct instruction: Teach them**—Provide clear and concise instruction on the lesson's content. This involves explaining new concepts, demonstrating skills, and presenting information in a structured way. Visual aids, examples, and analogies can be beneficial here.

- **Guided practice: Let them practice**—Let students practice the new skill or concept with the teacher's guidance. This can involve group activities, discussions, or hands-on exercises, and you can provide immediate feedback and support.

- **Independent practice: Let them practice alone**—To reinforce their learning, allow students to practice independently. This can include homework assignments, individual projects, or exercises that enable students to apply what they've learned without direct teacher assistance.

- **Monitoring of progress and learning: Determine if they learned it**—Plan how to evaluate whether students learned what you taught them. You can use quizzes, tests, oral presentations, or other formative and summative assessment forms. Assessments should align with the lesson objectives.

- **Closure: Call it a lesson**—Summarize the lesson and reinforce key points. This could involve a brief review where you ask students to share what they learned, or a reflective activity for consolidating their understanding.

- **Reflection: Ponder, "I taught it, so how did it go?"**—After the lesson, take time to reflect on what worked well and what can be improved. This self-assessment helps in refining future lesson plans and teaching practices.

- **High-interest reading materials:** Have articles or other reading materials copied and ready to go in case a lesson goes too quickly and you have time to fill. You can read the article to the students or have them read it independently or with a partner. Then, discuss the article as a class, and if there is time, ask students to write or draw a summary of the article. A powerful resource for lesson creation is ReadWorks (www.readworks.org), where you can download free articles that are appropriate for different grade levels.

When you create engaging and interesting lessons, your time spent as the main educator will go smoother, and students won't miss a beat in their learning.

### Artificial Intelligence for Lesson Ideas

Artificial intelligence (AI) has become a significant asset for teachers (and paraprofessionals) for lesson planning and lesson ideas. A great advantage of using AI in lesson design is its ability to generate resources quickly. AI chatbots such as ChatGPT and Google Gemini, to name just a few, can suggest lesson plans, create worksheets, and even develop interactive activities based on learning objectives. For example, these AI applications can analyze curriculum standards and recommend instructional strategies, saving you time in planning and creating while ensuring lessons align with educational goals. They can also assist you in differentiating instruction by providing various levels of difficulty for assignments to meet your students' diverse needs.

If you feel you are struggling to design a lesson, turn to an AI chatbot and ask it to be your thought partner. Let's say you are teaching a lesson on the solar system and have hit a roadblock in your planning. Here are some sample questions you could ask the chatbot to get you going.

- "What are some engaging ways to introduce the topic of the solar system to different age groups?"

- "How can I differentiate a solar system lesson for students with limited English proficiency?"

- "How can I scaffold vocabulary related to the solar system for multilingual learners?"

- "What are some hands-on or interactive activities to teach about planets and their characteristics?"

- "Can I provide exit ticket questions to gauge student understanding of the solar system?"

### Interactive Lesson Design

When you are designing a lesson, you need to decide what instructional strategies to use. It is critical that your superhero toolbox includes many different types of lessons, strategies, and activities to keep students engaged in their learning. The more engaged that students are, the fewer behavioral issues there will be, and the more enjoyable teaching will become. Try different strategies, keeping the ones that work well for you and the students and discarding the others. If students are engaged, they will not have time to for negative, attention-seeking behaviors.

- **Interactive discussions:** Encourage student-led discussions with open-ended questions that spark curiosity and critical thinking. Use debates, Socratic seminars, or fishbowl discussions to allow students to explore topics in depth while practicing respectful dialogue and reasoning skills. Talking circles or think-aloud activities can help younger students articulate their thoughts.

- **Hands-on activities:** Hands-on learning keeps students actively involved in the lesson. Activities such as science experiments, model building, and simulations allow students to connect concepts to the real world. Manipulatives like base 10 blocks, tangrams, and fraction strips in mathematics help make abstract concepts more tangible. In social studies, students might recreate historical events through dioramas or timelines.

- **Technology integration:** Make learning more interactive and dynamic with technology. Virtual field trips (such as Google Arts & Culture expeditions or NASA's Mars rover simulations) bring distant places into the classroom. Educational apps like Kahoot!, Wayground, or Nearpod turn review sessions into engaging experiences. Students can also create their own presentations using Canva or Prezi to demonstrate their learning.

- **Collaborative learning:** Students learn best from each other, so create opportunities for peer discussions, think-pair-share activities, and cooperative learning groups. Jigsaw activities, where each student becomes an "expert" on one piece of a topic and then teaches it to their peers, deepen comprehension and engagement. Group projects encourage teamwork and accountability while letting students take ownership of their learning.

- **Gamification:** Incorporate game-based learning to make lessons more motivating and interactive. Use escape rooms, trivia games, and classroom competitions to reinforce key concepts. Digital tools like Gimkit, Blooket, and Prodigy allow students to learn through play. Implement classroom reward systems, where students earn points, badges, or privileges for participation and achievements.

- **Project-based learning:** Encourage deep, meaningful learning by designing projects that require research, planning, and creativity. A science project on renewable energy, a history documentary on a historical figure, and a business plan for an entrepreneurial venture are real-world applications that promote critical thinking and problem solving.

- **Storytelling and role plays:** Narratives help students connect with content on a deeper level. Use historical reenactments, character hot seats, or storytelling exercises to make lessons memorable. Have students take on roles (for example, a scientist presenting a discovery, a lawyer defending a historical figure, or a news reporter covering an event) to bring the material to life.

- **Visual aids:** Infographics, anchor charts, concept maps, and diagrams are powerful tools for visual learners. Use graphic organizers like Venn diagrams, cause-and-effect charts, and flowcharts to help students structure their thinking. Digital tools like Padlet and Canva can help students create their own visual summaries.

- **Movement and kinesthetic learning:** Encourage physical movement to keep students engaged. Gallery walks, scavenger hunts, and interactive simulations provide opportunities for active participation. Programs like GoNoodle offer quick brain breaks to re-energize students. Incorporate hands-on experiments, role plays, and station rotations to get students moving.

- **Student choice and voice:** Letting students have a say in their learning increases engagement and motivation. Offer choices in projects, presentation formats, and even topics for research or writing. You can allow students to set personal learning goals and reflect on their progress through self-assessments or journaling.

- **Learning stations:** Set up multiple stations around the room, each with a different activity, reading, or experiment related to the lesson. Make sure to go over what signal you will use to let students know when it is time to rotate to the next station. Clearly explain what each station encompasses and the expectations for student behavior and work products. Some examples include the following.

  - A reading station with an article on the topic you are teaching

  - A hands-on station with a related experiment

  - A tech station where students explore an interactive website

  - A writing station where students reflect on what they learned

By incorporating a mix of these instructional strategies and activities, you can create dynamic and engaging lessons that cater to different learning preferences and keep students actively involved in their learning process.

## Relationship Building and Enjoyment of the Experience

> At the end of the day, focus on developing a positive rapport with students to create a supportive and trusting environment.

At the end of the day, focus on developing a positive rapport with students to create a supportive and trusting environment. Some students will need additional care because they feel fearful or anxious that their regular classroom teacher is not present. Gently reassure these students that you are here to help them and keep things running smoothly until their teacher can return. Enjoy the experience of being the primary teacher in the classroom, and don't be afraid to experiment with different teaching styles, voices, and activities. You can learn as you go!

## From Paraprofessional to Teacher: A Step-by-Step Guide

If stepping into the lead role feels like a good fit, you may be ready to take the next step in your education career. Transitioning from a paraprofessional to a certified teacher is a natural progression that builds on the practical skills and insights you've gained from hands-on classroom experience. You've already developed strengths in managing a classroom, supporting diverse learners, and collaborating with educators—essential qualities of an effective teacher. This foundation gives you a strong advantage when moving into a teaching role, as you have firsthand insight into student behavior, engagement, and instructional strategies. Since you already know you love working with students, becoming a teacher is a natural next step. Here are some practical steps you can take to go from paraprofessional to classroom teacher.

### *Explore Your Teaching Pathway*

Decide which teaching credential best aligns with your career goals.

- **Multiple-subject credential:** This is a credential for teaching elementary school (grades preK–6).

- **Single-subject credential:** This is a credential for teaching middle or high school in a specific subject area.

- **Special education credential:** This is a credential for working with students with disabilities at all grade levels.

- **Private school teaching:** Some private schools do not require a credential, meaning you can gain teaching experience there while you're pursuing certification.

---

### ACTION STEPS

1. Research the different types of credentials available.
2. Decide what type of credential you want to earn.
3. Discuss that type of credential with other educators to gain a deeper understanding of it.

---

### *Research Credential Programs*

There are several pathways to earning a teaching credential. Find the one that best fits your schedule and learning preference.

- **Traditional university programs:** You may enter a full-time, in-person program at a college or university.

- **Online or hybrid programs:** Flexible options can allow you to continue working while completing teaching coursework.

- **District, state, or provincial credentialing programs:** Some school districts offer programs that allow you to become a teacher while working as a paraprofessional.

---

**ACTION STEPS**

1. Research credential requirements for your state or province (visit its department of education's or ministry of education's website).
2. Compare program options and costs to find the best fit.
3. Consider financial aid, grants, or tuition reimbursement programs for school employees.

---

### Gain Teaching Experience While You Transition

There are several ways to gain teaching experience while you work as a paraprofessional.

- **Work as a substitute teacher:** If your district allows it, becoming a substitute teacher while completing your credential provides valuable classroom experience.

- **Teach in a private school:** If you're eager to start teaching right away, private schools often hire teachers without credentials. This can be a great stepping stone while you complete certification.

- **Request additional responsibilities:** Ask your administrator if you can lead small-group instruction, co-teach, or take on more classroom leadership tasks to gain experience.

---

**ACTION STEPS**

1. Apply for substitute teaching permits if your state or province allows paraprofessionals to sub.
2. Reach out to private schools in your area to inquire about teaching positions.
3. Speak with your principal or mentor teacher about taking on leadership opportunities.

---

### *Pass Required Exams*

Most states and provinces require prospective teachers to pass specific exams to earn a credential.

- **State- or province-specific exams:** These tests assess general teaching knowledge and subject-area expertise. You can find information about these exams on the website of your state's department of education, your province's ministry of education, or the state or provincial department that oversees teacher credentialing.

- **Basic skills and subject-matter competency tests:** Many states and provinces require these tests for admission to credential programs.

---

**ACTION STEPS**

1. Identify which exams are required by your state or province for your credential type.
2. Take practice tests and enroll in test prep courses if needed.
3. Register for and schedule your exams early to stay on track.

---

### *Complete Student Teaching and Credential Requirements*

Most programs require a semester or more of student teaching under the supervision of a mentor teacher. Some alternative programs allow you to work as a teacher while completing coursework.

---

**ACTION STEPS**

1. Work closely with your credential program to secure a student teaching placement.
2. Observe and learn from experienced teachers, asking for mentorship and feedback.
3. Document your experiences and reflections to build a strong teaching portfolio.

---

*Apply for Teaching Positions*

Once you've completed your credential, you're ready to apply for full-time teaching positions!

---

**ACTION STEPS**

1. Update your résumé and highlight your experience as a paraprofessional.
2. Gather letters of recommendation from teachers and administrators.
3. Search district job postings and attend education job fairs.

---

Your experience as a paraprofessional has given you a strong foundation for teaching. By taking strategic steps, researching credential programs, gaining teaching experience, passing exams, and completing student teaching, you can successfully transition into a rewarding career as a teacher. Education needs passionate, dedicated professionals like you, and this journey is just the beginning of making an even greater impact on students' lives!

## Reflection on Your Role as an Educational Paraprofessional

As a superhero paraprofessional, you have an essential role in shaping students' success, whether you work in special education, preschool, bilingual education, technology, behavioral intervention, or other specialized areas. Taking time to reflect on your work allows you to recognize your strengths, identify areas for growth, and ensure that you are maintaining a healthy balance between your professional responsibilities and your personal well-being. Here are some practical actions to guide you in your reflection practice. These are just suggestions. Find what works for you, knowing what is important is that you take time to practice reflection to continue to grow.

- **Assess your strengths and impact.**
  - Keep a reflection journal to document moments when you made a difference in a student's learning or behavior.
  - Ask yourself, "What strategies have worked well? Where have I seen the most progress in my students?"

- **Identify areas for growth.**
  - ✦ Set professional goals, like improving classroom management, learning new instructional strategies, or developing stronger communication skills.
  - ✦ Observe experienced paraeducators and teachers, and take notes on techniques of theirs that could enhance your practice.
- **Evaluate your work-life balance.**
  - ✦ Ask yourself, "Am I making time for self-care? Do I feel energized or overwhelmed by my work?"
  - ✦ Set boundaries by leaving work at work—avoid taking on more than you can handle. When you find yourself thinking about a work issue while you are at home, recognize that the issue literally came home with you. Kindly tell it that it can go back to school and that you will see it tomorrow.
- **Celebrate your wins, big and small.**
  - ✦ Recognize and appreciate your hard work. Your efforts may not always be acknowledged, but they are making a difference.
  - ✦ Share successes with your colleagues to build a supportive work environment.

By taking this time to reflect, you'll not only strengthen your skills as a paraprofessional but also ensure that you remain passionate and effective in your role. Your students and colleagues will thank you for it!

## Meet Ms. Lopez: Stepping Up as the Main Educator

Ms. Lopez, a dedicated paraprofessional, has been working at Jefferson Middle School for three years. She is well respected by her colleagues and students for her caring nature and strong organizational skills. One morning, the school principal informs her that she needs to serve as the primary educator for Ms. Russell's seventh-grade class for the day due to an emergency. Although initially taken aback by the sudden responsibility, Ms. Lopez quickly regains her composure. She understands the importance of maintaining a structured and supportive learning environment and decides to rely on the established classroom rules and routines to ensure a smooth day. Ms. Lopez jumps right in and does the following.

- **She greets students warmly and reinforces classroom rules:** Ms. Lopez emphasizes showing respect, listening, and staying on task.

- **She reviews the daily schedule:** Ms. Lopez ensures students understand and follow their familiar routine.

- **She starts the day with a morning meeting:** Ms. Lopez encourages students to share something positive to create a supportive atmosphere.

- **She uses the teacher's lesson plans:** Ms. Lopez makes minor adjustments for clarity and engagement.

- **She prepares materials ahead of time:** Ms. Lopez organizes resources and sets up the classroom for smooth transitions.

- **She incorporates interactive activities:** Ms. Lopez uses group discussions and hands-on projects to maintain engagement.

- **She offers encouragement and praise:** Ms. Lopez provides positive reinforcement to boost student confidence.

Ms. Lopez successfully navigates the day, demonstrating leadership and adaptability. The students respond well to her guidance and adhere to the rules and routines she reinforces. By showing genuine care and maintaining a well-organized classroom environment, Ms. Lopez ensures students have a productive and positive learning experience.

At the end of the school day, Ms. Lopez reflects on her experience. She realizes the importance of preparation, clear communication, and a caring attitude in managing a classroom effectively. Her success in stepping up as the lead educator boosts her confidence and reinforces her value as an essential member of the educational team at Jefferson Middle School.

## Wrap-Up

This chapter provided guidance and practical suggestions to prepare you for situations where you may need to step into the role of the main educator in the classroom. While these situations may not happen often, it's important to be ready. You now have strategies for building lesson plans, managing the classroom, and leading instruction when needed. In the feature box that follows, you'll find practical advice from experienced paraprofessionals who have taken on this role. Their insights are grounded in day-to-day experience. Then, in the "Notes and Reflections: Serving as the Main Educator" reproducible (page 156), you'll have the opportunity to thoughtfully reflect on what you've learned and consider how these insights apply to your own practice.

## *Advice From*
### SUPERHERO PARAPROFESSIONALS

"Preparation is key. Even if you don't have the exact lesson plans, having a clear structure and a backup plan makes a huge difference."

(K. Hoffman, personal communication, October 30, 2024)

"Recess and lunch are good opportunities to check in on students to say hello. Catch the student doing something right and let them know you see them. It is a game changer when students know they are seen and heard."

(B. O'Brien, personal communication, November 6, 2024)

"Being the primary teacher can be tricky. The students know you are not the main teacher, and they may challenge you and push back a bit. Show your confidence while also building a relationship with them. When they trust you and feel supported, they're more likely to stay engaged and on track."

(K. Burton, personal communication, October 20, 2024)

## Notes and Reflections: Serving as the Main Educator

Take a few moments to reflect on the following questions about being a superhero paraprofessional.

1. How can you better prepare for unexpected situations where you might need to take on the primary educator role?

2. How can you design engaging lesson plans to assist you in your teaching experience?

3. What strategies can you implement to maintain a structured and positive classroom environment?

4. Who are the key people you can turn to for support and advice in your school?

5. What steps can you take to develop your teaching style and confidence as an educator?

# 8

# Ensuring Self-Care and Continuing to Grow

The job of a superhero paraprofessional is filled with challenges that test both your strength and your heart. Your days are spent in the trenches, working tirelessly to support students with diverse learning needs and behavioral challenges, pouring your energy, patience, and empathy into their success. Emotional resilience is your superpower, allowing you to connect deeply with students who are facing personal or academic hurdles. You navigate complex emotional landscapes with sensitivity and care, offering support and hope in moments of uncertainty.

But wait, there's more! You wear many hats, each carrying a different responsibility. From guiding classroom instruction to providing specialized support in reading and mathematics, conducting assessments, and nurturing social skill development, you embody versatility and adaptability. You face new challenges each day

## KEY POINTS

- Prioritize self-care.
- Personalize your self-care.
- Become a lifelong learner.
- Use AI to keep growing.
- Go from paraprofessional to teacher.

and are constantly learning and growing in your knowledge and skills. If one thing is clear, it's this: To continue showing up as the superhero your students need, you must take care of yourself, and you must keep learning!

> To continue showing up as the superhero your students need, you must take care of yourself, and you must keep learning!

By focusing on self-care and lifelong learning, you can avoid burning out and stay in love with your profession. Self-care looks different for everyone, and we'll explore the many ways you can recharge and protect your well-being. We'll also discuss the importance of continuously growing in your career because education is a field with endless opportunities, and your potential is limitless. Let's dive in!

## Recognition of Burnout

In the fast-paced and sometimes stressful environment of a classroom, it is important that you recognize the signs of burnout in both yourself and your students. Burnout can manifest in various ways, including exhaustion, irritability, and a lack of motivation. For educators, unchecked burnout can decrease job satisfaction and effectiveness with students in the classroom. An essential superhero skill in education is learning to recognize the early signs so you can address burnout before it affects your well-being and performance.

One key sign of burnout is a feeling of emotional exhaustion. This may feel like a loss of enthusiasm for your work, trouble concentrating, or increased frustration with students or coworkers. You may also experience physical symptoms of burnout, such as headaches, stomachaches, or trouble sleeping. It is important to pay attention to these signs and seek support from colleagues, supervisors, or mental health professionals if needed.

A key strategy for preventing or dealing with burnout is to create a healthy work-life balance (Maslach & Leiter, 2016). This begins with effective time management, where prioritizing tasks and setting realistic daily goals can significantly reduce stress. You can use planners or digital calendars to organize work duties, and personal commitments can help you ensure that you give both work and life adequate attention. Make time for activities that promote relaxation and mental health, such as exercise or hobbies, and spend time with loved ones. By balancing work responsibilities and personal well-being, you can better serve your students and avoid burnout.

It's possible to be dedicated to your work, your family, and your personal interests all at once. The key is balance. Check in with yourself regularly and make adjustments when one area begins to overwhelm the others. A powerful way to protect yourself from burnout is to practice intentional self-care (Maslach & Leiter, 2016).

## A Paraprofessional's Guide to Self-Care

Every superhero has a source of strength. Superman recharges from the sun, Wonder Woman has her Amazonian training, and even Batman, for all his grit, relies on moments of solitude in the Batcave. As a paraprofessional, your power lies in your ability to support students with patience, adaptability, and compassion. But what happens when your energy runs low? Without self-care, even the mightiest heroes can burn out.

Self-care is not a luxury but a necessity. Research from the American Psychological Association shows that chronic stress without adequate recovery can lead to burnout, emotional exhaustion, and decreased job performance (Maslach & Leiter, 2016). However, when educators engage in regular self-care, they experience increased job satisfaction and improved emotional resilience (Jennings & Greenberg, 2009). Just as a superhero sharpens their skills, you must invest in self-care so that you can show up as your best self—for both your students and yourself.

> Self-care is not a luxury but a necessity.

This process begins with knowing your origin story. Every hero has one, something that drives them (their purpose). What recharges you? What drains you? Research on self-compassion highlights that individuals who tailor self-care to their unique needs are more likely to sustain it long-term (Neff & Germer, 2018). A simple way to start is by tracking your energy throughout the day. When do you feel your best? What small actions make a difference?

Self-care is not a one-size-fits-all approach. Because self-care is an individual journey, it requires us to become students ourselves and identify what refreshes us. For some, an energizing morning routine sets the tone for the day. For others, winding down with a book or soft music at night is key. The more you understand your personal needs, the stronger your self-care routine becomes.

Such routines are vital because superheroes don't wait until their powers fail before they take action. They train, prepare, and consistently maintain their strength. Your mission, should you choose to accept it, is to integrate self-care into your daily routine. Start small—one mindful breath during class transitions, one gratitude note at the end of the day, and one moment of laughter with a student. These small actions compound over time, reinforcing your resilience and ensuring that your heroic work continues not just for today but for years to come. A well-rounded self-care practice is like the ultimate superhero suit. Here are the important parts of the superhero suit.

### Physical Self-Care

Prioritizing sleep, hydration, and movement gives you the endurance to tackle each day. Whether this self-care involves taking a walk after work, breathing deeply, stretching between transitions, or fueling up with nutritious meals, your body needs maintenance to keep up with the demands of the job. Physical rejuvenation plays a vital role in reducing stress and enhancing overall well-being. Even short bouts of physical activity can improve your mood, boost cognitive function, and reduce anxiety by promoting the release of endorphins and enhancing blood flow to the brain (Frith & Loprinzi, 2018). Movement serves as a natural reset, helping individuals feel more energized and focused. Incorporating regular physical activity into daily routines can be a simple yet effective way to support both mental and physical health.

Rest and restoration are also essential for overall well-being, as they let the body and mind recover from daily stressors. Research highlights that adequate sleep improves cognitive function, emotional regulation, and physical health, while chronic sleep deprivation is linked to increased risks of anxiety, depression, and cardiovascular disease (Walker, 2017). Additionally, incorporating restful activities—such as mindfulness, nature walks, or simple breaks—can enhance productivity and reduce burnout (Sonnentag & Fritz, 2014). Prioritizing rest isn't just about relaxation; it's a fundamental component of sustaining long-term health and effectiveness in your personal and professional lives.

### Emotional Self-Care

Working with children and adolescents can be emotionally taxing. Journaling, going to therapy, or simply debriefing with a trusted colleague can provide much-needed emotional release. Engaging in creative outlets such as writing, painting, or playing music can be a powerful way to process emotions and enhance well-being. Creative expression is linked to reduced stress, improved mood, and increased psychological resilience (Stuckey & Nobel, 2010). Activities like journaling or art making provide means of self-reflection, allowing you to externalize thoughts and emotions in a constructive way and foster emotional healing, personal growth, and a greater sense of fulfillment.

### Social Self-Care

No hero fights alone. Friends, family, or fellow paraprofessionals offer a support system that prevents isolation. Meaningful social interactions, such as spending time with loved ones, engaging in meaningful conversations, or sending thoughtful messages, can significantly enhance psychological well-being. Social support from a spouse and friends is strongly associated with increased happiness and reduced depressive symptoms. When basic psychological needs, such as autonomy and relatedness, are satisfied, mental health can flourish (Shin & Park, 2022). Being and staying connected to others sharpens your superhero tools!

### Mental Self-Care

Just as superheroes need a strategy, you need mental clarity. Reading, engaging in creative hobbies, or practicing mindfulness can keep your mind sharp and focused. Incorporating mindfulness practices such as journaling, meditation, or quiet moments of self-reflection can effectively manage stress and enhance overall well-being. A 2018 randomized controlled trial found that employees who participated in a six-week mindfulness training program experienced significant reductions in both perceived and momentary stress compared to those who received a single-day training. The study suggests that more intensive mindfulness training may be necessary to improve workplace well-being outcomes (Chin, Slutsky, Raye, & Creswell, 2018). By integrating regular mindfulness techniques into daily routines, you can better manage stress and maintain a present-focused mindset, ultimately supporting your personal well-being and happiness.

### Spiritual Self-Care and Indulgence in Small Joys

Whether through meditation, prayer, or time in nature, grounding yourself in something bigger than day-to-day stressors can give you perspective and peace. Indulging in small joys can significantly enhance your sense of well-being by providing moments of comfort and relaxation. Research suggests that engaging in simple, pleasurable activities—such as enjoying a favorite snack, sipping tea, or watching a comfort show—can trigger the release of dopamine, a neurotransmitter associated with pleasure and stress relief (The Optimist Daily Editorial Team, 2025). These small acts of self-care serve as effective coping strategies, regulating your emotions and improving your overall mood. Prioritizing moments of joy can lead to a more balanced and fulfilling daily routine.

One helpful concept that highlights the power of small, positive actions is known as "joy snacking" (National Institute of Integrative Psychology, 2025). Joy snacking involves engaging in short activities that spark a sense of happiness or calm, like sharing a laugh with a friend, stepping outside for a few minutes of fresh air, or doodling in a notebook. These brief moments can trigger the release of dopamine as well. The more intentional you are about sprinkling these "snacks" of joy into your day, the more likely you are to feel grounded, energized, and emotionally well.

### The Power of Setting Boundaries

Setting boundaries is crucial for maintaining well-being and preventing burn-out. A lack of boundaries between work and your personal life can contribute to chronic stress and exhaustion (Maslach & Leiter, 2016). Recognizing personal limits and learning to say no can help you protect your mental and emotional energy. Additionally, reducing screen time and carving out personal time allow for meaningful rest and rejuvenation. Communicating needs to colleagues and supervisors fosters a supportive environment where it is easier to seek help when necessary. Prioritizing boundaries is not just an act of self-care but a strategy for long-term resilience and productivity.

Self-care involves engaging in activities that bring you joy and relaxation. Whether these include reading a book, going for a walk, or spending time with loved ones, you need to prioritize activities that replenish your energy and bring you happiness. Take time to figure out exactly what you need to keep your superhero skills strong.

## Lifelong Growth for Paraprofessionals

Another way to stay positively engaged in your paraprofessional career is to embrace lifelong learning. This can involve several different activities and habits, and you need to decide how you want to keep learning. Learning more about something you are interested in is a surefire way to stay enthusiastic for your job and for your students.

To continue to evolve as a professional, you may seek educational opportunities that will give you more tools for your superhero toolbox. Trainings, articles, and books can help you stay current in the field of education and advance your career. Whether you are a special education paraprofessional, a bilingual paraprofessional, or any other educational paraprofessional, various options are available to help you learn and grow in this profession. The following sections explore a few of these.

### Taking Online Courses or Completing a Certification Program

An option to continue your learning is to take online courses or complete a certification program. Online courses offer flexibility and convenience, allowing you to learn at your own pace and on your own schedule. Certification programs can provide a more structured approach to learning and may lead to additional credentials or qualifications that can enhance your résumé and open up new opportunities for advancement. Some potential training topics to explore include the following.

- **Understanding of diverse learning needs:** You can learn about strategies for supporting students with various learning disabilities and developmental disabilities, such as dyslexia, ADHD, autism, and others.

- **Behavior management and support:** You can learn techniques for managing classroom behavior, including positive reinforcement, de-escalation strategies, and behavioral intervention plan development.

- **Assistive technology:** You can learn how to use various assistive technologies that support students with disabilities, such as text-to-speech software, communication devices, and adaptive tools.

- **Instructional strategies and differentiation:** You can learn techniques for modifying and differentiating instruction to meet the diverse needs of students.

- **Cultural competency:** You can focus on how to understand and respect diverse cultural backgrounds and how cultural differences impact learning and behavior.

- **Emergency response and safety procedures:** You can learn about what to do in certain emergencies.

There are so many different topics to learn more about. Once you start, you will want to keep learning!

### Leveraging AI for Learning

As a paraprofessional, you can harness the power of AI to support your ongoing professional development. Whether you're looking for ideas to assist in lesson planning, strategies to support diverse learners, or ways to better understand classroom management techniques, AI can serve as a helpful thought partner. You can also use AI to explore behavior strategies, generate questions for student check-ins, or find culturally responsive resources. By using AI as a learning and planning companion, you can gain a wide range of ideas and tools that may help you feel more confident and prepared in your role while you continue to grow professionally.

For example, you can ask AI questions such as the following.

- **"What strategies can I use to support a student with [specific learning disability or developmental disability] in the classroom?"** AI can provide tailored strategies and accommodations to help address specific needs, whether for students with dyslexia, ADHD, autism, or other conditions.

- **"Can you suggest engaging and educational activities for students struggling with [specific subject or skill]?"** AI can recommend interactive and practical activities that cater to students' needs and help make learning more engaging and effective.

- **"How can I create a behavior management plan for a student exhibiting [specific behavioral issues]?"** AI can offer advice on developing a behavior management plan, including techniques for positive reinforcement and strategies for addressing specific behavioral challenges.

- **"What are some accessible tools and technologies that can assist students with [specific needs or disabilities]?"** AI can provide information about various assistive technologies and tools to help students with physical, sensory, or cognitive disabilities engage more effectively in their education.

- **"How can I differentiate instruction to meet the diverse needs of students in my classroom?"** AI can offer strategies for differentiating instruction, including ways to modify lessons, provide alternative resources, and use various teaching methods to accommodate different learning preferences and abilities.

- **"How can I deal positively with stress and tiredness?"** AI can offer great strategies and suggestions to deal proactively with stress and exhaustion and take good care of yourself.

The potential for misuse is broad, but when used thoughtfully, AI can enhance learning, streamline tasks, and provide valuable support in lesson planning, differentiation, and student engagement. While AI should complement—not replace—human insight and creativity, it offers opportunities to personalize instruction, generate resources, and improve efficiency.

### Advancing Your Career in Education

Networking and building professional relationships are essential components of success in education. As a superhero paraprofessional, you play a critical role in supporting student learning, and developing strong connections with colleagues, administrators, and other education professionals can enhance your impact. By taking the following networking steps, you actively open doors to professional growth, career advancement, and valuable resources and insights that can help you navigate the evolving landscape of education.

1. **Engage in professional development.**

   - Attend workshops, conferences, and seminars to expand your knowledge, learn best practices, and stay updated on the latest educational trends. A good starting point is the National Resource Center for Paraeducators, Related Service Providers, and Interveners, which hosts a virtual national conference each year.

   - Participate in webinars and virtual training sessions if in-person events are inaccessible.

   - Ask your administrator or lead teacher about training opportunities that could benefit your role.

2. **Join professional organizations and online communities.**

   - Become a member of education associations such as the National Education Association or local paraprofessional organizations.

   - Engage in social media groups, discussion forums, or LinkedIn communities dedicated to paraprofessionals and educators.

   - Subscribe to education newsletters and podcasts to stay informed about new research, policies, and strategies. Visit the websites of organizations such as the Paraprofessional Resource and Research Center (PAR²A Center; https://paracenter.org) or the Council for Learning Disabilities (https://council-for-learning-disabilities.org) to access resources.

3. **Foster relationships within your school community.**

   - Build strong partnerships with teachers by offering collaboration and sharing insights on student progress.

   - Seek mentorship from experienced educators who can guide you along your career path.

   - Connect with administrators and support staff to better understand schoolwide initiatives and advocate for professional growth opportunities.

4. **Take on leadership and growth opportunities.**

   - Volunteer for school committees, extracurricular activities, or curriculum-planning teams to gain experience beyond the classroom.

- Consider cross-training in different educational areas, such as special education or education for multilingual learners, to broaden your skill set.

- Express interest in career-advancement pathways, such as becoming a certified teacher, behavior specialist, or interventionist.

Networking isn't just about advancing your career. It's about learning from others, sharing knowledge, and contributing to a community of educators who are all working toward the same goal: student success. By actively engaging in professional relationships, you can gain new perspectives, discover career opportunities, and find inspiration to continue growing in your role.

## Meet Sarah: Supporting Yourself With Self-Care

Sarah is a dedicated paraprofessional in a high school special education classroom. She has been in this role for five years and has developed strong bonds with her students and colleagues. Her typical day involves assisting the teacher with lesson implementation, providing one-on-one support to students with special needs, and ensuring a positive and inclusive classroom environment.

One day, Sarah faces several challenges at work. One of her students has a behavioral outburst that requires her to de-escalate the situation while maintaining the safety of other students. Additionally, administrative changes in the classroom procedures add to the stress of the day. When Sarah returns home, she feels emotionally drained and mentally exhausted.

Recognizing the importance of self-care, Sarah makes a deliberate effort to prioritize her well-being before returning to work the next day. Here's how she approaches her self-care routine.

- Sarah starts her evening with a relaxing yoga session. Yoga helps her release physical tension and unwind after a challenging day. The gentle stretches and deep breathing exercises allow her to reconnect with her body and relax.

- After yoga, Sarah journals about her day. Writing down her thoughts and emotions helps her reflect on the day's events and gain perspective. It allows her to acknowledge her frustration and find constructive ways to address it.

- Sarah contacts a close friend for a casual phone call. Connecting with someone outside of work who understands her challenges provides her with emotional support and reassurance. It reminds her that she is not alone in facing difficult situations and that sharing experiences can be therapeutic.

- Before bed, Sarah practices mindfulness meditation. She focuses on her breath and practices being present in the moment. Mindfulness meditation helps her quiet her mind and let go of lingering stressors from the day; this promotes a sense of calm and inner peace.

- Sarah makes sure she gets a full night's rest by establishing a bedtime routine. An hour before bed, she avoids screens, dims the lights, and reads a relaxing book. Quality sleep is crucial for her to recharge both physically and mentally.

The following morning, Sarah wakes up feeling refreshed. Her self-care practices have effectively replenished her energy and resilience. She approaches the new day at work with a positive mindset and a renewed sense of purpose. She is able to handle challenges more calmly and is better equipped to support her students and collaborate with her colleagues. Sarah's commitment to self-care benefits her personal well-being and enhances her effectiveness as a paraprofessional.

## Wrap-Up

This chapter offered guidance on how to prioritize self-care while continuing to grow personally and professionally. You now have strategies for maintaining your well-being, managing stress, and seeking out opportunities for ongoing learning and development. In the feature box that follows, you'll find practical advice from experienced paraprofessionals who have embraced these practices. Their insights are grounded in day-to-day experience. Then, in the "Notes and Reflections: Ensuring Self-Care and Continuing to Grow" reproducible (page 169), you'll have the opportunity to thoughtfully reflect on what you've learned and consider how these insights apply to your own practice.

## *Advice From*
### SUPERHERO PARAPROFESSIONALS

"I've learned that caring for myself allows me to bring my best self to work daily. It's not selfish; it's necessary for everyone's benefit, especially the students."

(B. Nicholson, personal communication, September 29, 2024)

"Investing in professional development shows my commitment to growth and improving my skills, which directly benefits the students I work with. It also helps me feel fueled for the job."

(L. Frere, personal communication, November 2, 2024)

"You are not 'just' a paraprofessional. You are important!"

(H. Hopple, personal communication, January 20, 2025)

# Notes and Reflections: Ensuring Self-Care and Continuing to Grow

Take a few moments to reflect on the following questions about being a superhero paraprofessional.

1. Reflect on a time when you felt overwhelmed or stressed at work. How did you manage those emotions, and what self-care strategies did you employ to regain balance?

2. Which self-care strategies resonate with you the most, and how do you plan to incorporate them into your daily or weekly schedule?

3. How do you see self-care contributing to your effectiveness and resilience as a paraprofessional?

4. What steps can you take to grow in your profession?

5. What skills or knowledge have you gained as a paraprofessional, and how have your experiences as a paraprofessional shaped your aspirations for the future?

# The Power of Your Work

As we come to the end of this book, one truth remains clear: Paraprofessionals are the heart of our classrooms and schools. Your role as a paraprofessional is not just about providing assistance—it's about shaping lives, fostering confidence, and ensuring every student has the support they need to succeed. Paraprofessionals are the compassionate guides, the unwavering advocates, and the creative problem solvers who make learning accessible for all. While your work may sometimes go unnoticed, its impact is undeniable. You are not just supporting education—you are transforming it.

Reflecting on my own journey from paraprofessional to principal, I can say with certainty that the lessons I learned as a paraprofessional prepared me for every step that followed—becoming a teacher, a leader, and even a parent. The skills you develop in this profession will serve you in ways you cannot yet imagine. Education is a path of growth, both for your students and for you. Whether you continue as a paraprofessional or you pursue new opportunities, know that the work you do today is shaping the future, one student at a time.

Maya Angelou is quoted as saying in a speech, "People will forget what you said, people will forget what you did, but people will never forget how you made them feel." As a paraprofessional, you make students feel seen, valued, and capable. You create a safe space where they can learn, grow, and believe in themselves. That is your superpower.

So, as you move forward on your journey, embrace the challenges, continue to learn, and never forget the incredible impact you have. The world of education is better because of you. Thank you for your dedication, your passion, and your unwavering commitment to making a difference. You are a superhero, and our schools are lucky to have you!

# References and Resources

Ablon, J. S. (2020, January 9). School discipline is trauma-insensitive and trauma-uninformed [Blog post]. *Psychology Today*. Accessed at www.psychologytoday.com/us/blog/changeable /202001/school-discipline-is-trauma-insensitive-and-trauma-uninformed on July 6, 2025.

ADHD Centre. (2022, July 21). *Successful people with ADHD superpowers* [Blog post]. Accessed at www.adhdcentre.co.uk/successful-people-with-adhd-superpowers on October 13, 2024.

American Academy of Pediatrics. (2022, November 15). *Eating disorders and the school setting*. Accessed at https://www.aap.org/en/patient-care/school-health/mental-health-in-schools /eating-disorders-and-the-school-setting on April 25, 2025.

American Psychological Association. (2020, March 4). *Working out boosts brain health*. Accessed at www.apa.org/topics/exercise-fitness/stress on January 12, 2025.

American Speech-Language-Hearing Association. (n.d.). *Child speech and language*. Accessed at www.asha.org/public/speech/disorders/childsandl on April 25, 2025.

Americans With Disabilities Act of 1990, 42 U.S.C. § 12101 et seq. (1990).

Apter, A. (2014). Adolescent self-harm: New horizons? *Journal of the American Academy of Child and Adolescent Psychiatry, 53*(10), 1048–1049.

Ashbaker, B. Y., & Morgan, J. (2015). *The paraprofessional's guide to effective behavioral intervention*. Routledge.

Bailey, B. A. (2001). *Conscious discipline: Seven basic skills for brain smart classroom management*. Loving Guidance.

Bailey, K., & Nelson, K. (2024). *The successful substitute: How to prepare, grow, and flourish as a guest teacher*. Solution Tree Press.

Balfanz, R., & Byrnes, V. (2021, December). *Connecting social-emotional development and academic indicators across multiple years.* Everyone Graduates Center, Johns Hopkins University School of Education. Accessed at www.cityyear.org/wp-content/uploads /2022/06/20220203_EGC_CityYearReport2_BalfanzByrnes.pdf on September 3, 2025.

Barkley, R. A. (2013). *Taking charge of ADHD: The complete, authoritative guide for parents* (3rd ed.). Guilford Press.

Better Kid Care. (2024, April 3). *Pave the way for self-regulation and problem-solving with social-emotional learning.* Penn State Extension. Accessed at https://extension.psu.edu /programs/betterkidcare/news/pave-the-way-for-self-regulation-and-problem-solving-with -social-emotional-learning on August 9, 2025.

Birsh, J. R., & Carreker, S. (Eds.). (2018). *Multisensory teaching of basic language skills* (4th ed.). Brookes.

Blank, C., & Shavit, Y. (2016). The association between student reports of classmates' disruptive behavior and student achievement. *AERA Open, 2*(3). https://doi.org/10.1177 /2332858416653921

Blasey, J., Wang, C., & Blasey, R. (2022). Accommodation use and academic outcomes for college students with disabilities. *Psychological Reports, 126*(4), 1891–1909.

Brock, M. E. (2021). A tiered approach for training paraeducators to use evidence-based practices for students with significant disabilities. *Teaching Exceptional Children, 54*(3), 224–233.

Bunford, N., Evans, S. W., & Wymbs, F. (2015). ADHD and emotion dysregulation among children and adolescents. *Clinical Child and Family Psychology Review, 18*(3), 185–217. https://doi.org/10.1007/s10567-015-0187-5

CAST. (2024). *Universal Design for Learning guidelines version 3.0.* Author. Accessed at https://udlguidelines.cast.org on August 29, 2025.

Causton, J., & MacLeod, K. (2021). *The paraprofessional's handbook for effective support in inclusive classrooms* (2nd ed.). Brookes.

Cavanaugh, B. (2013). Performance feedback and teachers' use of praise and opportunities to respond: A review of the literature. *Education and Treatment of Children, 36*(1), 111–137.

Centers for Disease Control and Prevention. (2022). *What is ADHD?* Accessed at www.cdc .gov/ncbddd/adhd/facts.html on August 29, 2025.

Centers for Disease Control and Prevention. (2024, May 16). *Signs and symptoms of autism spectrum disorder.* Accessed at www.cdc.gov/autism/signs-symptoms/index.html on November 20, 2024.

Centers for Disease Control and Prevention. (2025, June 5). *Data and statistics on children's mental health.* Accessed at www.cdc.gov/children-mental-health/data-research on April 25, 2025.

Children and Adults with Attention-Deficit/Hyperactivity Disorder. (n.d.). *Parenting a child with ADHD.* Accessed at https://chadd.org/for-parents/overview on August 29, 2025.

Childs, K. E., Kincaid, D., George, H. P., & Gage, N. A. (2015). The relationship between school-wide implementation of Positive Behavior Intervention and Supports and student discipline outcomes. *Journal of Positive Behavior Interventions, 18*(2), 89–99. https://doi .org/10.1177/1098300715590398

Chin, B., Slutsky, J., Raye, J., & Creswell, J. D. (2018). Mindfulness training reduces stress at work: A randomized controlled trial. *Mindfulness, 10*(4), 627–638.

Cipriano, C., Strambler, M. J., Naples, L. H., Ha, C., Kirk, M., Wood, M., et al. (2023). The state of evidence for social and emotional learning: A contemporary meta-analysis of universal school-based SEL interventions. *Child Development, 94*(5), 1181–1204.

Clay, R. A. (2020). Self-care has never been more important. *Monitor on Psychology, 51*(5), 60. Accessed at www.apa.org/monitor/2020/07/self-care on April 27, 2025.

Cohen, R. K., Opatosky, D. K., Savage, J., Stevens, S. O., & Darrah, E. P. (2021). *The metacognitive student: How to teach academic, social, and emotional intelligence in every content area.* Solution Tree Press.

Collaborative for Academic, Social, and Emotional Learning. (n.d.). *Fundamentals of SEL.* Accessed at https://casel.org/fundamentals-of-sel on April 25, 2025.

Colorado Department of Education. (2023). *English language development guidebook: Designing, delivering, and evaluating instruction and services for multilingual learners.* Author. Accessed at www.cde.state.co.us/cde_english/eldguidebook on August 29, 2025.

Consiglio, B. (2021, February 22). *Focus on the positive to improve classroom behavior.* University of Missouri. Accessed at https://showme.missouri.edu/2021/focus-on-the -positive-to-improve-students-classroom-behavior on December 5, 2024.

Council for Exceptional Children. (2022, March 16). *Core competencies for special education paraeducators.* Accessed at https://exceptionalchildren.org/paraeducators/core-competencies -special-education-paraeducators on January 22, 2025.

Creswell, J. D. (2017). Mindfulness interventions. *Annual Review of Psychology, 68,* 491– 516. https://doi.org/10.1146/annurev-psych-042716-051139

Davis, T. (2018, December 28). Self-care: 12 ways to take better care of yourself [Blog post]. *Psychology Today.* Accessed at www.psychologytoday.com/us/blog/click-here-happiness /201812/self-care-12-ways-take-better-care-yourself on January 15, 2025.

Denham, S. A., Bassett, H. H., & Wyatt, T. (2015). The socialization of emotional competence. In J. E. Grusec & P. D. Hastings (Eds.), *Handbook of socialization: Theory and research* (2nd ed., pp. 590–613). Guilford Press.

DePaoli, J. L., Atwell, M. N., & Bridgeland, J. (2017, November). *Ready to lead: A national principal survey on how social and emotional learning can prepare children and transform schools.* CASEL. Accessed at https://casel.org/ready-to-lead on December 3, 2024.

Dong, Z., Liu, H., & Zheng, X. (2021). The influence of teacher-student proximity, teacher feedback, and near-seated peer groups on classroom engagement: An agent-based modeling approach. *PLoS ONE, 16*(1), Article e0244935. https://doi.org/10.1371/journal .pone.0244935

D'Orio, W. (2023). To fix students' bad behavior, stop punishing them: Collaborative methods for handling misconduct make their way to the classroom. *Education Next*, *23*(4), 50–55.

DuFour, R., DuFour, R., Eaker, R., Many, T. W., Mattos, M., & Muhammad, A. (2024). *Learning by doing: A handbook for Professional Learning Communities at Work* (4th ed.). Solution Tree Press.

DuPaul, G. J., & Stoner, G. (2014). *ADHD in the schools: Assessment and intervention strategies* (3rd ed.). Guilford Press.

Dweck, C. S. (2006). *Mindset: The new psychology of success*. Random House.

Dweck, C. (2017). *Mindset—Updated edition: Changing the way you think to fulfil your potential*. Little, Brown Book Group.

Echevarría, J., Vogt, M., & Short, D. J. (2017). *Making content comprehensible for English learners: The SIOP model* (5th ed.). Pearson.

Education 360 Journal. (2024, February 11). Why your school needs paraprofessional support for students with disabilities. *Medium*. Accessed at https://education360journal .medium.com/why-your-school-needs-paraprofessional-support-for-students-with -disabilities-75b7f3d3c265 on December 30, 2024.

Elbertson, N. A., Jennings, P. A., & Brackett, M. A. (2025). The role of educators in school-based social and emotional learning. *Social and Emotional Learning: Research, Practice, and Policy*, *6*, Article 100134. https://doi.org/10.1016/j.sel.2025.100134

Fink, G. (2023, June). *What is assets-based teaching and how does it enable equity practices in college classrooms?* [Blog post]. Every Learner Everywhere. Accessed at www.everylearner everywhere.org/blog/what-is-assets-based-teaching-and-how-does-it-enable-equity-practices -in-college-classrooms on January 20, 2025.

Fisher, D., & Frey, N. (2021). *Better learning through structured teaching: A framework for the gradual release of responsibility* (3rd ed.). ASCD.

Fletcher, J. M., Lyon, G. R., Fuchs, L. S., & Barnes, M. A. (2019). *Learning disabilities: From identification to intervention* (2nd ed.). Guilford Press.

Flexibility. (n.d.) In *Oxford English dictionary*. Accessed at https://doi.org/10.1093/ OED/9907100328 on November 21, 2025.

Flint, A. S., & Jaggers, W. (2021). You matter here: The impact of asset-based pedagogies on learning. *Theory Into Practice*, *60*(3), 254–264. https://doi.org/10.1080/00405841.2021 .1911483

Florio, J. (2024, December 1). *12 astonishing facts about paraprofessional educators*. Accessed at https://facts.net/general/12-astonishing-facts-about-paraprofessional-educator on September 2, 2025.

Frey, N., Fisher, D., & Smith, D. (2022). *The social-emotional learning playbook: A guide to student and teacher well-being*. Corwin.

Frith, E., & Loprinzi, P. D. (2018). Physical activity is associated with higher cognitive function among adults at risk for Alzheimer's disease. *Complementary Therapies in Medicine, 36,* 46–49.

Gabriel, R., & López, F. (2024). The role of asset-based pedagogy in an interactive view of reading. *Educational Psychologist, 59*(4), 233–249. https://doi.org/10.1080/00461520 .2024.2394031

Garcia, A. (2021, April 2). *New study reveals positive impacts of paraeducators on student achievement* [Blog post]. New America. Accessed at www.newamerica.org/education -policy/edcentral/new-study-reveals-positive-impacts-of-paraeducators-on-student -achievement on April 28, 2025.

Garey, J. (2025, August 4). *Mindfulness in the classroom: How it helps kids regulate behavior and focus on learning.* Child Mind Institute. Accessed at https://childmind.org/article /mindfulness-in-the-classroom on September 2, 2025.

Gavin, M. L. (2018, June). *Autism factsheet (for schools).* Nemours KidsHealth. Accessed at https://kidshealth.org/en/parents/autism-factsheet.html on January 8, 2025.

Gerszberg, C. O. (n.d.). *Best practices for bringing mindfulness into schools.* Mindful. Accessed at www.mindful.org/mindfulness-in-education on February 1, 2025.

Gilmour, A. F., Sandilos, L. E., Pilny, W. V., Schwartz, S., & Wehby, J. H. (2022). Teaching students with emotional/behavioral disorders: Teachers' burnout profiles and classroom management. *Journal of Emotional and Behavioral Disorders, 30*(1), 16–28. https://doi .org/10.1177/10634266211020258

Girard-Joyal, O., & Gauthier, B. (2021). Creativity in the predominantly inattentive and combined presentations of ADHD in adults. *Journal of Attention Disorders, 26*(9), 1187–1198.

Goodwin, A. K. B., & Long, A. C. J. (2022). Parents' perceptions of culturally responsive teacher practices and elementary children's mental health and well-being. *Journal of Child and Family Studies, 32*(1), 781–795. https://doi.org/10.1007/s10826-022-02454-3

Gray, C. (2015). *The new Social Story book, revised and expanded: Over 150 social stories that teach everyday social skills to children and adults with autism and their peers* (15th anniversary ed.). Future Horizons.

Graziano, P. A., & Garcia, A. (2016). Attention-deficit hyperactivity disorder and children's emotion dysregulation: A meta-analysis. *Clinical Psychology Review, 46,* 106–123.

Greenberg, M. T. (2023, March 6). *Evidence for social and emotional learning in schools* [Brief]. Learning Policy Institute. Accessed at https://learningpolicyinstitute.org/product /evidence-social-emotional-learning-schools-brief on February 24, 2025.

Hagelskamp, C., Brackett, M. A., Rivers, S. E., & Salovey, P. (2013). Improving classroom quality with the RULER Approach to Social and Emotional Learning: Proximal and distal outcomes. *American Journal of Community Psychology, 51*(3–4), 530–543.

Hannigan, J., & Djabrayan Hannigan, J. (2024). *Behavior academies: Targeted interventions that work!* Solution Tree Press.

Hattie, J. (2023). *Visible learning: The sequel—A synthesis of over 2,100 meta-analyses relating to achievement.* Routledge.

Hawken, L. S., Vincent, C. G., & Schumann, J. (2020). Systemic implementation of schoolwide positive behavior interventions and supports in urban schools: Promoting equity in discipline. In L. Simonsen & D. Freeman (Eds.), *Supporting behavior for school success* (pp. 33–52).

Hierck, T., & Weber, C. (2025). *Positive behaviors start with positive mindsets: Twenty-eight actions to motivate students and boost achievement.* Solution Tree Press.

Hoffmann, J. D., Brackett, M. A., Bailey, C. S., & Willner, C. J. (2020). Teaching emotion regulation in schools: Translating research into practice with the RULER approach to social and emotional learning. *Emotion, 20*(1), 105–109.

Hoshaw, C. (2022, March 29). *What is mindfulness? A simple practice for greater well-being.* Healthline. Accessed at www.healthline.com/health/mind-body/what-is-mindfulness on April 28, 2025.

Individuals With Disabilities Education Act, 20 U.S.C. § 1400 (2004).

IRIS Center. (n.d.). *Addressing challenging behaviors (part 1, elementary): Understanding the acting-out cycle* [Module]. Peabody College, Vanderbilt University. Accessed at https://iris .peabody.vanderbilt.edu/module/bi1-elem/challenge/#content on July 28, 2024.

Jangmo, A., Stålhandske, A., Chang, Z., Chen, Q., Almqvist, C., Feldman, I., et al. (2019). Attention-deficit/hyperactivity disorder, school performance, and effect of medication. *Journal of the American Academy of Child and Adolescent Psychiatry, 58*(4), 423–432.

Jennings, P. A., & Greenberg, M. T. (2009). The prosocial classroom: Teacher social and emotional competence in relation to student and classroom outcomes. *Review of Educational Research, 79*(1), 491–525. https://doi.org/10.3102/0034654308325693

Jimerson, S. R., Nickerson, A. B., Mayer, M. J., & Furlong, M. J. (Eds.). (2012). *Handbook of school violence and school safety: International research and practice* (2nd ed.). Routledge.

Johns Hopkins Medicine. (n.d.). *Oppositional defiant disorder (ODD) in children.* Accessed at www.hopkinsmedicine.org/health/conditions-and-diseases/oppositional-defiant-disorder on December 12, 2024.

Jones, B. T., Erchul, W. P., & Geraghty, C. A. (2021). Supplemental reading interventions implemented by paraprofessionals: A meta-analysis. *Psychology in the Schools, 58*(4), 723–741.

Katz, S. B. (2025). *The SWIRL method: Supporting multilingual learners as they speak, write, interact, read, and listen.* Solution Tree Press.

Kemp, G., Smith, M., & Segal, J. (2025, January 20). *Learning disabilities and disorders in children.* Accessed at www.helpguide.org/family/learning-disabilities/learning-disabilities -and-disorders on September 2, 2025.

Kofler, M. J., Soto, E. F., Fosco, W. D., Irwin, L. N., Wells, E. L., & Sarver, D. E. (2020). Working memory and information processing in ADHD: Evidence for directionality of effects. *Neuropsychology, 34*(2), 127–143.

Kroska, E. B., Roche, A. I., & O'Hara, M. W. (2018). Childhood trauma and somatization: Identifying mechanisms for targeted intervention. *Mindfulness, 9*, 1845–1856. https://doi.org/10.1007/s12671-018-0927-y

Kusché, C. A., & Greenberg, M. T. (2012). The PATHS Curriculum: Promoting emotional literacy, prosocial behavior, and caring classrooms. In S. R. Jimerson, A. B. Nickerson, M. J. Mayer, & M. J. Furlong (Eds.), *Handbook of school violence and school safety: International research and practice* (2nd ed., pp. 435–446). Routledge.

Kuypers, L. M. (2011). *The Zones of Regulation: A curriculum designed to foster self-regulation and emotional control.* Think Social.

Laceulle, O. M., Kleber, R. J., & Alisic, E. (2015). Children's experience of posttraumatic growth: Distinguishing general from domain-specific correlates. *PLoS ONE, 10*(12), Article e0145736. https://doi.org/10.1371/journal.pone.0145736

Lawson, G. M., McKenzie, M. E., Becker, K. D., Selby, L., & Hoover, S. A. (2019). The core components of evidence-based social emotional learning programs. *Prevention Science: The Official Journal of the Society for Prevention Research, 20*(4), 457–467.

Lemov, D., Hernandez, J., & Kim, J. (2016). *Teach like a champion field guide 2.0: A practical resource to make the 62 techniques your own.* Jossey-Bass.

Lewis, B. A. (2021). *Social emotional stories: Lessons and learning from plants and animals.* Free Spirit.

Lin, L., Parker, K., & Horowitz, J. M. (2024, April 4). *Challenges in the classroom.* Pew Research Center. Accessed at www.pewresearch.org/social-trends/2024/04/04/challenges-in-the-classroom on February 3, 2025.

Loe, I. M., & Feldman, H. M. (2007). Academic and educational outcomes of children with ADHD. *Journal of Pediatric Psychology, 32*(6), 643–654.

Maki, E., Shaw, S., Putnam, R., Harrington, E., & Schrieber, S. (2022, August). *Supporting students with autism spectrum disorders through school-wide positive behavior interventions and supports.* Center on PBIS. Accessed at https://www.pbis.org/resource/supporting-students-with-autism-spectrum-disorders-through-school-wide-positive-behavior-interventions-and-supports on November 21, 2025.

Malesu, V. K. (2024, April 21). Childhood trauma linked to higher rates of somatic symptoms, study finds. *News-Medical.* Accessed at www.news-medical.net/news/2024 0421/Childhood-trauma-linked-to-higher-rates-of-somatic-symptoms-study-finds.aspx on August 29, 2025.

Margolis, M. J., & Feinberg, R. A. (Eds.). (2020). *Integrating timing considerations to improve testing practices.* Routledge.

Marzano, R. J. (2005). *Building background knowledge for academic achievement: Research on what works in schools*. ASCD.

Maslach, C., & Leiter, M. P. (2016a). Burnout. In G. Fink (Ed.), *Stress: Concepts, cognition, emotion, and behavior* (pp. 351–357). Academic Press. https://doi.org/10.1016/B978-0-12-800951-2.00044-3

Maslach, C., & Leiter, M. P. (2016b). Understanding the burnout experience: Recent research and its implications for psychiatry. *World Psychiatry, 15*(2), 103–111. https://doi.org/10.1002/wps.20311

Mattos, M., Buffum, A., Malone, J., Cruz, L. F., Dimich, N., & Schuhl, S. (2025). *Taking action: A handbook for RTI at Work*™ (2nd ed.). Solution Tree Press.

McCurdy, B. H., Scozzafava, M. D., Bradley, T., Matlow, R., Weems, C. F., & Carrion, V. G. (2023). Impact of anxiety and depression on academic achievement among underserved school children: Evidence of suppressor effects. *Current Psychology, 42*, 26793–26801. https://doi.org/10.1007/s12144-022-03801-9

McKeown, M. G. (2019). Effective vocabulary instruction fosters knowing words, using words, and understanding how words work. *Language, Speech, and Hearing Services in Schools, 50*(4), 466–476.

Mental Health First Aid USA. (2022, March 14). *How and why to practice self-care*. Accessed at www.mentalhealthfirstaid.org/2022/03/how-and-why-to-practice-self-care on October 21, 2024.

Merrick, M. T., Ford, D. C., Ports K. A., Guinn, A. S., Chen, J., Klevens, J., et al. (2019). Vital signs: Estimated proportion of adult health problems attributable to adverse childhood experiences and implications for prevention—25 states, 2015–2017. *Morbidity and Mortality Weekly Report, 68*(44), 999–1005.

Minahan, J., & Rappaport, N. (2012). *The behavior code: A practical guide to understanding and teaching the most challenging students*. Harvard Education Press.

Moore, D. A., Russell, A. E., Matthews, J., Ford, T. J., Rogers, M., Ukoumunne, O. C., et al. (2018). School-based interventions for attention-deficit/hyperactivity disorder: A systematic review with multiple synthesis methods. *Review of Education, 6*(3), 209–263.

Moya, M. S., Caldarella, P., Larsen, R. A. A., Warren, J. S., Bitton, J. R., & Feyereisen, P. M. (2022). Addressing adolescent stress in school: Perceptions of a high school wellness center. *Education and Treatment of Children, 45*(3), 277–291.

Myers, D. M., Simonsen, B., & Sugai, G. (2011). Increasing teachers' use of praise with a response-to-intervention approach. *Education and Treatment of Children, 34*(1), 35–39.

National Association of School Psychologists. (2020). *A framework for effective school discipline*. Author. Accessed at www.nasponline.org/disciplineframework on August 4, 2025.

National Center for Chronic Disease Prevention and Health Promotion. (2017). *Addressing the needs of students with chronic health conditions: Strategies for schools* [Research brief]. Centers for Disease Control and Prevention. Accessed at https://archive.cdc.gov/# /details?url=https://www.cdc.gov/healthyschools/chronic_conditions/pdfs/2017_02_15 -How-Schools-Can-Students-with-CHC_Final_508.pdf on April 28, 2025.

National Institute for Play. (n.d.). *The importance of play for adults.* Accessed at https://nif play.org/play-note/adult-play on August 4, 2025.

Neff, K., & Germer, C. (2018). *The mindful self-compassion workbook: A proven way to accept yourself, build inner strength, and thrive.* Guilford Press.

Nelson, K. (1999). *Developing students' multiple intelligences, grades K–8.* Scholastic.

The Optimist Daily Editorial Team. (2025, June 12). *Why little treats matter: The science-backed benefits of small daily joys.* The Optimist Daily. Accessed at www.optimistdaily.com /2025/06/why-little-treats-matter-the-science-backed-benefits-of-small-daily-joys on August 9, 2025.

Orvell, A., Kross, E., & Gelman, S. A. (2020). Talking about emotions: Distanced self-talk enhances emotional regulation across childhood. *Child Development, 91*(3), 960–975.

Paterson, J. (2022, June 9). New focus on strength-based learning. *NEA Today.* Accessed at www.nea.org/nea-today/all-news-articles/new-focus-strength-based-learning on December 20, 2024.

Pearson, P. D., & Gallagher, M. C. (1983, October). *The instruction of reading comprehension* (Technical Report No. 297). Center for the Study of Reading.

Perry, B. D., & Szalavitz, M. (2017). *The boy who was raised as a dog: And other stories from a child psychiatrist's notebook* (Rev. & updated ed.). Basic Books.

Pisacreta, J., Tincani, M., Connell, J. E., & Axelrod, S. (2011). Increasing teachers' use of a 1:1 praise-to-behavior correction ratio to decrease student disruption in general education classrooms. *Behavioral Interventions, 26*(4), 243–260.

Price, C. J., & Hooven, C. (2018). Interoceptive awareness skills for emotion regulation: Theory and approach of mindful awareness in body-oriented therapy (MABT). *Frontiers in Psychology, 9,* Article 798.

Prothero, A. (2023, April 20). Student behavior isn't getting any better, survey shows. *Education Week.* Accessed at www.edweek.org/leadership/student-behavior-isnt-getting -any-better-survey-shows/2023/04 on April 28, 2025.

Reflection Sciences. (n.d.). *Executive function, ADHD, and academic success.* Accessed at https://reflectionsciences.com/research-spotlight-executive-function-adhd-and-academic -success on August 29, 2025.

Reibel, A. R. (2023). *Embracing relational teaching: How strong relationships promote student self-regulation and efficacy.* Solution Tree Press.

Rush, S. E., & Sharma, M. (2016). Mindfulness-based stress reduction as a stress management intervention for cancer care: A systematic review. *Journal of Evidence-Based Complementary and Alternative Medicine, 22*(2), 348–360.

Santiago-Rosario, M. R., McIntosh, K., Izzard, S., Cohen Lissman, D., & Calhoun, E. (2023, September). *Is Positive Behavioral Interventions and Supports (PBIS) an evidence-based practice?* Center on PBIS. Accessed at www.pbis.org/resource/is-school-wide-positive-behavior-support-an-evidence-based-practice on February 6, 2025.

Sayal, K., Prasad, V., Daley, D., Ford, T., & Coghill, D. (2018). ADHD in children and young people: Prevalence, care pathways, and service provision. *The Lancet Psychiatry, 5*(2), 175–186. https://doi.org/10.1016/S2215-0366(17)30167-0

Schaeffer, K. (2023, July 24). *What federal education data shows about students with disabilities in the U.S.* Pew Research Center. Accessed at www.pewresearch.org/short-reads/2023/07/24/what-federal-education-data-shows-about-students-with-disabilities-in-the-us on December 28, 2024.

Schonert-Reichl, K. A., & Roeser, R. W. (Eds.). (2016). *Handbook of mindfulness in education: Integrating theory and research into practice.* Springer.

Shaywitz, B. A., & Shaywitz, S. E. (2020). The American experience: Towards a 21st century definition of dyslexia. *Oxford Review of Education, 46*(4), 454–471.

Shin, H., & Park, C. (2022). Social support and psychological well-being in younger and older adults: The mediating effects of basic psychological need satisfaction. *Frontiers in Psychology, 13*, Article 1051968.

Sisson, C. (2022, December 16). *The benefits of differentiation in the classroom* [Blog post]. HMH. Accessed at https://www.hmhco.com/blog/benefits-of-differentiation-in-the-classroom on January 14, 2025.

Sonnentag, S., & Fritz, C. (2014). Recovery from job stress: The stressor-detachment model as an integrative framework. *Journal of Organizational Behavior, 36*(1), S72–S103. https://doi.org/10.1002/job.1924

Stapleton-Corcoran, E. (2022, February 12). *Universal design for learning (UDL).* Center for the Advancement of Teaching Excellence, University of Illinois Chicago. Accessed at https://teaching.uic.edu/cate-teaching-guides/inclusive-equity-minded-teaching-practices/universal-design-for-learning-udl on November 17, 2024.

Stuckey, H. L., & Nobel, J. (2010). The connection between art, healing, and public health: A review of current literature. *American Journal of Public Health, 100*(2), 254–263.

Substance Abuse and Mental Health Services Administration. (2014, July). *SAMHSA's concept of trauma and guidance for a trauma-informed approach* (HHS Publication No. SMA 14-4884). U.S. Department of Health and Human Services. Accessed at https://www.health.ny.gov/health_care/medicaid/program/medicaid_health_homes/docs/samhsa_trauma_concept_paper.pdf on August 8, 2025.

Swedo, E. A., Aslam, M. V., Dahlberg, L. L., Niolon, P. H., Guinn, A. S., Simon, T. R., et al. (2023). Prevalence of adverse childhood experiences among U.S. adults: Behavioral risk factor surveillance system, 2011–2020. *Morbidity and Mortality Weekly Report, 72*(26), 707–715.

Tamir, T. T., Tekeba, B., Mekonen, E. G., Gebrehana, D. A., & Zegeye, A. F. (2025). Shadows of trauma: An umbrella review of the prevalence and risk factors of post-traumatic stress disorder in children and adolescents. *Child and Adolescent Psychiatry and Mental Health, 19*(1), Article 48. https://doi.org/10.1186/s13034-025-00879-4

Taylor, R. D., Oberle, E., Durlak, J. A., & Weissberg, R. P. (2017). Promoting positive youth development through school-based social and emotional learning interventions: A meta-analysis of follow-up effects. *Child Development, 88*(4), 1156–1171.

Thompson, E. M., & Kirkwood, K. (2021). *Professional role of paraprofessionals: A literature review* [Master's thesis, Minnesota State University Moorhead]. Dissertations, Theses, and Projects. https://red.mnstate.edu/thesis/585

Tomlinson, C. A. (2014). *The differentiated classroom: Responding to the needs of all learners* (2nd ed.). ASCD.

Vaughn, S., & Bos, C. S. (2015). *Strategies for teaching students with learning and behavior problems* (9th ed.). Pearson.

Wagner, F., Wagner, R. G., Kolanisi, U., Makuapane, L. P., Masango, M., & Gómez-Oliyé, F. X. (2022). The relationship between depression symptoms and academic performance among first-year undergraduate students at a South African university: A cross-sectional study. *BMC Public Health, 22*(1), Article 2067.

Walker, M. (2017). *Why we sleep: Unlocking the power of sleep and dreams.* Scribner.

Walker, V. L., Douglas, K. H., Douglas, S. N., & D'Agostino, S. R. (2020). Paraprofessional-implemented systematic instruction for students with disabilities: A systematic literature review. *Education and Training in Autism and Developmental Disabilities, 55*(3), 303–317.

# Index

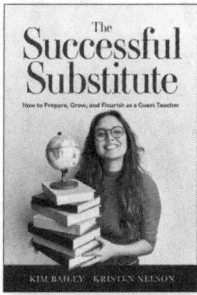

## Successful Substitute
### *Kim Bailey and Kristen Nelson*
Gain practical guidance on how to maintain effective classroom management while forming connections with students and advancing classroom content. Field-tested strategies and insights from substitute teachers will help prepare you for a day that is both enjoyable and productive.
**BKG145**

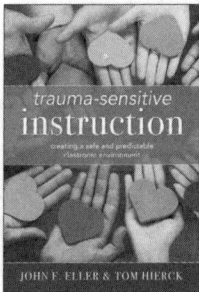

## Trauma Sensitive Instruction
### *John F. Eller and Tom Hierck*
Confidently and meaningfully support your trauma-impacted students with this accessible resource. The authors draw from their personal and professional experiences with trauma, mental health, and school culture to provide real insight into what you can do now to help learners build resilience and achieve at high levels.
**BKF847**

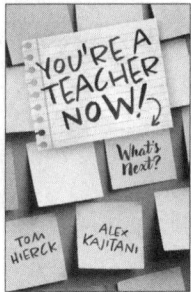

## You're a Teacher Now! What's Next?
### *Tom Hierck and Alex Kajitani*
Trusted education experts Tom Hierck and Alex Kajitani draw from their experiences to offer research-backed tools and strategies in an easily referenced FAQ format that both new and veteran teachers can use in their classrooms to address everything from behavior management to self-care planning.
**BKG142**

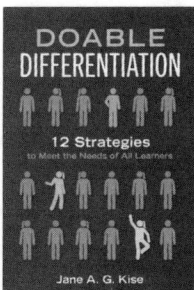

## Doable Differentiation
### *Jane A.G. Kise*
Differentiating for students' learning preferences can often seem too complex and complicated for too little gain. With Doable Differentiation, you will discover a series of straightforward, high-reward strategies that educators like you use daily to support, engage, and challenge students with diverse learning styles.
**BKF952**

Solution Tree | Press

a division of

Solution Tree

Visit SolutionTree.com or call 800.733.6786 to order.

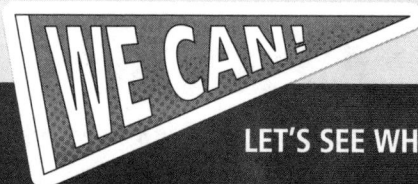